McGRAW-HILL EDUCATION

Conversational American English

The Illustrated Guide to the
Everyday Expressions of American English

McGRAW-HILL EDUCATION

Conversational American English

The Illustrated Guide to the Everyday Expressions of American English

RICHARD A. SPEARS • BETTY BIRNER • STEVEN KLEINEDLER

Illustrated by Luc Nisset

New York   Chicago   San Francisco   Athens   London   Madrid
Mexico City   Milan   New Delhi   Singapore   Sydney   Toronto

11 12 13 14 15 16 17 18 19 20 QFR 21 20 19 18 17

ISBN   978-0-07-174131-6
MHID   0-07-174131-3

e-ISBN 978-0-07-174132-3
e-MHID   0-07-174132-1

Library of Congress Cataloging-in-Publication Data

Spears, Richard A.
      McGraw-Hill Education: conversational American English / Richard Spears, Stephen R. Kleinedler, Betty J. Birner.
            p.   cm.
      ISBN 0-07-174131-3 (alk. paper)
      1. English language—United States—Conversation and phrase books.
2. English language—United States—Terms and phrases.   3. English language—Spoken English—United States.   4. Figures of speech.   5. Americanisms.
      I. Title.   II. Title: Conversational American English.

PE2839.S634   2010
423'.1—dc22   2010010886

McGraw-Hill Education products are available at special quantity discounts to use as premiums and sales promotions or for use in corporate training programs. To contact a representative, please visit the Contact Us pages at www.mhprofessional.com.

This book is printed on acid-free paper.

Contents

About This Dictionary

Every language has conventional and much-used ways of expressing even the most commonplace requests, inquiries, or responses. Some of these expressions are idioms or idiomatic. Others are perfectly understandable and literal English, but people unfamiliar with the language may have difficulty formulating them in typical and conventional ways. Derived from *NTC's Dictionary of Everyday American English Expressions*, this book is a collection of nearly 5,000 such expressions grouped into 464 topics that are listed under 11 major categories of social interaction. New to this reference are extensive illustrations that place numerous expressions in a visual context, facilitating understanding and memorization.

The complete list of major category headings and their topics can be found in the **Topic and Situation Index**, beginning on page xi. This index can also be used for browsing through the topics. See a complete explanation of how to use this index on page xi. Each of the 464 topics has been assigned a number, and these numbers are the basis of the indexing systems. The numbers appear at the beginning of each topic heading in the body of the book to aid in finding a particular topic.

Using This Dictionary

The meaning of the expressions can be determined from the topic heading. All the expressions under a particular heading convey essentially the same type of information.

- The expressions themselves contain hints and explanations where necessary. For instance, in the expression . . .

    I got sidetracked.
        sidetracked = detoured; distracted

    . . . the equal sign (=) indicates that the word or phrase on the left is defined as the word or phrase on the right.

- In the expression . . .

    Can you stay for dinner?
        Can you = Would you, Are you able to, Will you

    . . . the = indicates that the word or phrase on the left can be replaced by any of the words or phrases on the right.

- In the expression . . .

    Get off your high horse. (*informal*)
        = Be less arrogant.

    . . . the equal sign (=) at the beginning of the line indicates that a restatement of the entire expression follows.

- In the expression . . .

    > You and what army? (*slang*)

    . . . the word *slang* in parentheses indicates the register or usage of the expression. Other similar indicators are *Biblical, cliché, euphemistic, folksy, formal, French, German, idiomatic, informal, ironic, Italian, Japanese, jocular, juvenile, Latin, mild oath, mildly vulgar, oath, rude, sarcastic, Spanish, taboo,* and *vulgar.*

- In the expression . . .

    > Fore!
    >> (*said in golfing when the ball is struck*)

    . . . the information in parentheses explains something about the context in which the expression is used.

Topic and Situation Index

This index includes 11 major category headings, under which the topics for each category appear in boldface type. The specific expression groups for each topic are then presented in the order in which they are found in the list of expressions. A topic number, rather than a page number, is provided after each topic description, indicating where to find that topic in the list.

For instance, if you wanted to find an expression having to do with a pain in the head, you would look under the category **Personal Matters** for a group of expressions labeled **Sickness**. Under **Sickness** you would find the expression group "Describing a pain in the head **326**." Look for "Describing a pain in the head" at number 326 in the list of expressions.

Basic Social Encounters

Greetings

Disagreeing

Conversational Encounters

Focusing Attention

Launching the Conversation

Disputes

Discussion and Resolution

Polite Encounters

Prefaces

Communication Barriers

Telling Time

General Pleasantries

Business Pleasantries

Apologizing and Taking Responsibility

Forgiving

Showing Gratitude

Returning Thanks

Special Occasions

Impolite Encounters

Dealing with Unpleasantness

Visits

Guests and Hosts

Miscellaneous Expressions

Comments and Phrases

Plans and Projects

Personal Matters

Feelings

Anxiety

The Senses

Health and Appearance

Sickness

Family Matters

Home Life

Education

Children

Food and Drink

Restaurants

Bars

Home Cooking

Shopping

Stores and Shops

Telephones and Mobile Devices

Answering the Telephone

Conversational American English Expressions

BASIC SOCIAL ENCOUNTERS

Greetings

1   Simple greetings

Hi!
Hello!
Hello there!
Howdy!
Hey!
Yo! (*slang*)

2   General greetings

How are you?
How's it going?

How's it been?
How is everything?
How's everything?
How have you been?
How've you been?
How you been? (*informal*)
How's tricks? (*informal*)
What have you been up to?
What's new? (*informal*)
What's up? (*informal*)
Wusup? / Wassup? (*slang*)
What's happening? (*slang*)
What's going on? (*slang*)

3 Greetings for various times of the day

Good morning.
Morning.
Mornin'. (*informal*)
How are you this bright morning?
Good afternoon.
Afternoon.
Good evening.
Evening.

4 Greeting a person you haven't seen in a long time

I haven't seen you in years!
Long time no see! (*informal*)
I haven't seen you in an age!
I haven't seen you in a month
of Sundays!
a month of Sundays = a long time

5 Welcoming someone who has returned

Welcome back!

Welcome back, stranger!

Long time no see! (*cliché*)

Where were you?

Where have you been?

Where did you go?

6 Expressing surprise at meeting someone

What a surprise to meet you here!

Imagine meeting you here! (*cliché*)

Fancy meeting you here. (*cliché*)

Never thought I'd see you here!

What are you doing in this neck of the woods?

> *neck of the woods = part of town, location*

What are you doing in this part of town?

What are you doing out of the office?

Where've you been hiding yourself?

What have you been up to?

Shouldn't you be in school?

Shouldn't you be at work?

Have you been keeping busy?

You been keeping busy?

Been keeping busy?

7 After you have greeted someone

We seem to keep running into each other.

Haven't we met before?

We have to stop meeting like this. (*cliché*)

Didn't we meet at that party last week?

I'm sorry; I've forgotten your name.

I've been meaning to call you.

How was it?
How did it go?
Did everything go OK?
Did you have fun?
You'll have to tell us all about it.
Did you take any pictures?
Do you have pictures?
Were the locals friendly?
Were the natives friendly?
Did you bring me anything?
We missed you.
We missed you around here.
We've missed you around here.
It just wasn't the same without you.

Small Talk

9 Expressing your state of health and happiness

Fine.
I'm fine.
I'm cool. (*slang*)
Keeping cool.
Dandy. (*informal*)
Fine and dandy.
Great.
Couldn't be better.
Happy as a clam. (*cliché*)
Okay.
All right.
(I) can't complain.

No complaints.

I have nothing to complain about.

10   Telling how you have been doing—positive

Keeping busy.

Keeping myself busy.

Been keeping myself busy.

Keeping out of trouble.

Been keeping out of trouble.

Been up to no good. (*informal*)

Been keeping my nose clean. (*informal*)

11   Telling how you have been doing—neutral

Getting by.

Been getting by.

Fair to middling. (*folksy*)

So-so. (*informal*)

Plugging along. (*informal*)

Could be worse.

Could be better.

(Just) muddling through.

Same as always.

Same as usual.

Same o(l)' same o(l)' (*informal*)

12   Telling how you have been doing—negative

Not good.

Not so good.

Not too good.

None too good.

Not well.

Not very well.

Not so well.

Not too well.
None too well.
Not so hot.
Not too hot.
None too hot.
Not great.
Not so great.
None too great.
Crummy. (*slang*)
Kind of crummy. (*slang*)
Lousy. (*slang*)
I've seen better days.
I've had better days.
Could be better.
I've been better.
I've been under the weather.

I've seen better days.

13   Explaining that you have been busy

I'm busy.
Keeping busy.
Keeping myself busy.
Been keeping myself busy.
I'm swamped.

> *swamped = overwhelmed, as with a swamped boat*

I'm snowed under.

> *snowed under = as if buried in snow*

I don't have time to breathe.
I don't have time to think.
There aren't enough hours in the day.
Not a moment to spare.
I've been running around with my head cut off. (*informal*)
I've been running around like a chicken with its head cut off.

> (*informal*)

14 Inviting a friend for a drink or coffee

Do you have time for coffee?
How about a cup of coffee?
Let's go get coffee. Do you have any time?
Let's go for coffee.
Let's go for a beer.
Let's go for a drink.

Introductions

15 Introducing someone to someone else

I'd like you to meet my friend Mary.
I'd like you to meet Mary.
This is my friend Mary.
John, (this is) Mary. Mary, John.
Mary, have you met John?
Mary, do you know John?
Mary, shake hands with John Jones.
Do you two know each other?
Have you met?
Have you two been introduced?
Haven't you been introduced?
Oh, I'm sorry; how silly of me. This is Mary.
Mary, John is the guy I was telling you about. (*informal*)
You two have a lot in common.

Mary, have you met John?

16 When you have just been introduced to someone

Good to meet you.
Nice to meet you.
Nice meeting you.
How nice to meet you. (*formal*)

How very nice to meet you. (*formal*)

What a pleasure to meet you. (*formal*)

It's a pleasure to have finally met you. (*formal*)

I am pleased to make your acquaintance. (*formal*)

I'm happy to meet you.

I'm glad to meet you.

Glad to meet you.

Charmed. (*formal*)

A pleasure. (*formal*)

17   After you have been introduced to someone

I've been wanting to meet you for some time.

John has told me all about you.

John has told me so much about you.

I've heard so much about you.

I've heard so much about you I feel I know you already.

So we finally meet face to face.

We've exchanged e-mails; it's nice to meet in person.

I'm sorry, what was your name again?

I didn't catch your name. I'm terrible at names.

18   Asking how someone is

How are you?

How's your family?

How's the family?

How are you doing?

How are you doing today?

How you doing?

Are you doing OK?

How are you feeling?

How you feeling?

Are you feeling better today?

How have you been?

How you been?

19   Asking someone how things are going

How're things?
How're things with you?
How're things going?
How's with you?
How's by you? (*slang*)
How's business?
How's tricks? (*slang*)
How's it shakin'? (*slang*)
How's everything?
How's every little thing? (*folksy*)
How's everything going?
How's it going?
How goes it?
How goes it with you?
How are you getting on?
How are you getting along?
How's the world (been) treating you?

Ending a Conversation

20   Signaling the end of a conversation

Oh, look at the time!
It's getting later.
Well, David, it's really good to see you, but I really must go.
It's been fun talking to you.
(It's been) nice chatting with you.
It's so good to see you again.
We have to make plans to get together some time.
Let's do lunch sometime.

21　Ending a telephone conversation

I really have to go now. We'll talk sometime.
There's someone on the other line. I must say good-bye now.
The doorbell is ringing. I'll call you back.
Can I call you back? Something has come up.
I have to get back to my work. I'll call again later.
Can we continue this later? My other line is ringing.
I have to get back to work before the boss sees me.
I won't keep you any longer.
I'll let you go now.

> Can I call you back? Something has come up.

22　Ending a conversation abruptly

I'm going to have to run.
Must run. (*informal*)
I'm all out of time. I'll have to say good-bye now.
Look at the time. I really must go.
It's been great talking to you, but I have to go.
Wow! I'm late. Look, I'll call you.
Sorry, but I have to leave now.
Let's continue this another time. I really must go.

Good-Byes

23　Simple good-byes

Good-bye.
Bye.
Bye-bye.
So long.
Ta-ta. (*informal*)
Farewell.
Cheerio.

Hasta la vista. (*Spanish*)

Adios. (*Spanish*)

Auf wiedersehen. (*German*)

Sayonara. (*Japanese*)

Arrivederci. (*Italian*)

Au revoir. (*French*)

Adieu. (*French*)

Ciao. (*Italian*)

Good day. (*formal*)

Good evening. (*formal*)

Good night.

Good-bye until later.

Good-bye until next time.

Good-bye for now.

See you later.

See you later, alligator. (*slang*)

Later, gator. (*slang*)

Later. (*informal*)

I'll try to catch you later.

I'll catch you later.

Catch you later.

I'll talk to you soon.

Let's get together soon.

I'll be seeing you.

I'll see you real soon.

See you.

See ya. (*informal*)

See you soon.

See you real soon.

See you around.

See you in a little while.

See you next year.

See you then.

See you tomorrow.

Good running into you.

>   *running into you = meeting up with you*

Nice running into you.

Nice talking to you.

Take care.

(It was) good to see you.

(It was) nice to see you.

Nice meeting you.

It was a pleasure meeting you. (*formal*)

It is a pleasure to have met you. (*formal*)

It's been a real pleasure. (*formal*)

25   **Leaving a place**

Are we ready to leave?

Are you about finished?

Are you ready to go?

Ready to go?

Ready to roll? (*slang*)

Are we away? (*slang*)

Let's blow. (*slang*)

>   *blow = leave*

Let's get out of this taco stand. (*slang*)

>   *taco stand = a cheap place; an undesirable place*

Let's blow this joint. (*slang*)

>   *= Let's leave this place.*

Let's go while the going's good. (*cliché*)

>   *Let's = Time to, We've got to*

Let's get while the getting's good. (*cliché*)

Let's head out.

Let's beat a hasty retreat. (*cliché*)

Let's make tracks. (*informal*)

>   *make tracks = leave a trail (as we go)*

Let's motor. (*slang*)
> to motor = to leave by automobile

Let's hit the road. (*slang*)
Let's boogie. (*slang*)
Let's split. (*slang*)
Let's make like a tree and leave. (*jocular*)
Let's make like the wind and blow. (*jocular*)
Let's make like a banana and split. (*jocular*)
Exit stage right.
Exit stage left.
Retreat! (*slang*)

26   When someone is leaving on a journey

Bon voyage!
Have a good trip!
Have a nice flight.
Have a nice trip.
Have a safe trip.
Have a safe journey.
Drive carefully.
Take care of yourself.
Take care.
We'll miss you.
All the best.

27   Making plans to keep in touch with someone

I'll call you when I get home.
Call when you get there.
Don't forget to call.
Write me.
Let's write.
You've got my e-mail address?
Text me.

I'm on Facebook.

    Facebook = Twitter, MySpace, LinkedIn, etc.

Let's do lunch.

I'll be in touch.

Let's keep in touch.

Agreeing

28   Simple agreement

Yes.

Yeah. (*informal*)

Yep. (*informal*)

Yup. (*informal*)

Right.

You're right.

Right you are.

Right on!

Right-o.

Uh-huh.

Sure.

Sure thing.

You got it.

You bet.

Absolutely.

By all means.

29   Stating your concurrence

This is true.

That's true.

You're right.

Ain't that the truth?

Ain't it the truth?

That's right.
That's for certain.
That's for sure.
That's for darn sure.
That's for damn sure. (*mildly vulgar*)
Damn straight! (*mildly vulgar*)
It works for me.
Well said.
I agree.
I agree with you 100 percent.
I couldn't agree with you more.
I have no problem with that.
We see eye to eye on this.
I couldn't have said it better.
You took the words right out of my mouth.
I'll drink to that!

30   Expressing acceptance

It's fine.
I think it's fine.
It's good enough.
It's satisfactory.
It'll do.
It'll serve the purpose.
I like it.
I love it.
I think it's great.
I like the color.
I like the texture.
I like the flavor.
It's got a good rhythm.
It's wonderful.
It's fabulous.
It's ideal.
It's a masterpiece.

It's perfect.

It's A-1.

This is second to none.

This is perfect.

This is far and away the best.

This is the ultimate.

It couldn't be better.

Never been better.

There's none better.

It doesn't get any better than this.

I've never seen anything like it.

This is the cream of the crop. (*cliché*)

This is the pick of the litter. (*idiomatic*)

    litter = a group of newborn pups

This is the crème de la crème. (*cliché*)

    = *This is the best of the best.*

This is head and shoulders above the rest.

That suits me to a T.

    = *That suits me fine.*

That's the ticket. (*idiomatic*)

That's just what the doctor ordered. (*idiomatic*)

That's just what I needed.

That hits the spot. (*idiomatic*)

That fits the bill. (*idiomatic*)

That's it.

That's the greatest thing since sliced bread. (*cliché*)

It's in a league of its own.

I give it four stars.

It gets two thumbs up. (*idiomatic*)

I've hit the jackpot.

    jackpot = sum of money to be won in gambling

Bingo! (*slang*)

    = *I did it!*

Jackpot! (*slang*)

    = *I did it!; It is good!*

Bull's-eye! (*slang*)
Bonus score! (*slang*)

31   **Stating that you understand**

I hear you.
I hear you, man.
I hear what you're saying.
I see what you're saying.
I can see what you're saying.
I can see that.
I see what you mean.
I see where you're coming from.
I know.
I know what you mean.
Point well taken.
I know what you're talking about.
I understand what you're saying.
Understood.
I dig it. (*slang*)
I can dig it. (*slang*)
I got you.
Gotcha.
(I) got it.
I follow you.
I'm with you.
I'm there with you.
I've been there.
Read you loud and clear.
Roger.
Roger, wilco.
    wilco = will comply
Roger Dodger. (*slang*)

Do you know what I mean?

Do you know what I'm talking about?

Know what I mean?

Does that make any sense?

Am I making sense?

Are you following me?

Know what I'm saying?

You know?

Do you see what I mean?

See what I mean?

Don't you see?

Do you get the message?

Do you get the picture?

Get the message?

Get the picture?

Get my drift?

Do you get it?

Get it?

Do you follow?

Do you follow me?

Dig? (*slang*)

 = *Do you understand?*

Understand?

Do you understand?

Do you hear what I'm saying?

Do you hear me?

Do you see where I'm coming from?

 where I'm coming from = what my position is

Do you agree?

You're with me, right?

Are you with me on this?

Do we see eye to eye on this?

33   Stating simple disagreement or refusal

No.
Nope.
No way.
Not a chance.
Not! (*slang*)
Uh-uh.
I don't think so.

34   Stating categorical disagreement

That's not true.
That's not right.
You've got that wrong.
You've got it all wrong.
Wrong!
You missed the boat. (*idiomatic*)
You're missing the boat. (*idiomatic*)
Wrong on both counts.
You're wrong.
You're dead wrong.
You're off.
You're way off base.

35   Stating strong disagreement

I disagree completely.
I couldn't disagree (with you) more.
Horsefeathers! (*slang*)
Bullshit. (*taboo*)
That's BS. (*mildly vulgar*)
Bull. (*mildly vulgar*)
Baloney. (*slang*)

That's a load of crap. (*mildly vulgar*)
That's a lot of bull. (*mildly vulgar*)
That's a lot of baloney. (*slang*)
That's a bunch of baloney. (*slang*)
That's a bunch of malarkey. (*slang*)
Lies!
That's a lie.
That's a big, fat lie. (*informal*)
You're lying through your teeth.
Look me in the eye and say that.

36 Stating your disagreement with a proposition

That's out of the question.
That's unthinkable.
That's insane.
That doesn't even merit a response.
I'll give that all the consideration it's due.

37 Expressing rejection

I can't stand it.
I hate it.
I don't care for it.
I don't like it.
It's not my style.
It's not for me.
It stinks. (*informal*)
It sucks. (*mildly vulgar*)
It reeks. (*informal*)
My kid could do that.
It's awful.
It's terrible.
It's ugly.
It's hideous.
It's dreadful.

It's hell on earth. (*informal*)

I don't get it.

Don't quit your day job.

38   Expressing refusal

No.

Nope. (*informal*)

No way.

No way, José. (*informal*)

No can do. (*informal*)

No, sir.

No sirree. (*folksy*)

No sirree, Bob. (*folksy*)

Sorry.

Nothing doing.

You're out of luck.

In a pig's eye. (*idiomatic*)

When pigs fly. (*idiomatic*)

When hell freezes over. (*informal*)

There isn't a snowball's chance in hell. (*informal*)

Not a chance.

No chance.

Not if I can help it.

Not likely.

Not bloody likely. (*mildly vulgar*)

Absolutely not!

It will be a cold day in hell before I do that. (*informal*)

Only in your dreams.

Dream on.

Save your breath.

Save it.

You're barking up the wrong tree. (*idiomatic*)

Over my dead body. (*idiomatic*)

Forget it.

If you think that, you've got another think coming.

Not in a million years.
Not for a million dollars.
You couldn't pay me to do it.
Not in your wildest dreams.
You wish.
I'll be damned first. (*mildly vulgar*)
I'll be damned if I do. (*mildly vulgar*)
Damned if I will. (*mildly vulgar*)
Like hell. (*mildly vulgar*)
I'll see you in hell first. (*mildly vulgar*)

39 Stating that someone is wrong

What are you talking about?
You don't know what you're talking about.
You don't have a leg to stand on.
You haven't got a leg to stand on.
You don't know the first thing about it.
You're really stretching the truth.
You're way off base.
You can lay that notion to rest.

What are you talking about?

40 Arguing about the facts

You've got it all wrong.
You've got the facts wrong.
You've got your facts wrong.
You haven't got the facts.
You haven't got the facts right.
I don't think you've got your facts straight.
Don't speak until you've got your facts straight.
Next time get the facts straight. (*informal*)
Next time get the facts first. (*informal*)
Don't jump to conclusions.

CONVERSATIONAL ENCOUNTERS

Focusing Attention

41   Getting someone's attention

Pardon me. (*formal*)
Excuse me.
Hey! (*informal*)
Hey, you! (*informal*)
Yo! (*slang*)

42   Getting someone to listen to you

Look here. (*informal*)
Listen here. (*informal*)
Listen up. (*informal*)
Get a load of this. (*informal*)
Now hear this! (*informal*)
Hear me out.
Are you ready for this? (*informal*)
Listen. (*informal*)
Are you listening to me?
Are you paying attention?
I'm talking to you.
Do you hear me?
Do I have your ear? (*idiomatic*)
Can I bend your ear a minute? (*idiomatic*)
Am I making myself heard?

43   Directing attention to an object

Look at this.
Take a look at this.

Get a load of this.

Take a gander at that. (*informal*)
   a gander = a look

Feast your eyes on this.

Look what we have here.

Lookie here. (*informal*)

Lookit. (*slang*)

Look here.

Can you eyeball this (for a minute)? (*slang*)
   to eyeball = to look at

Can you believe your eyes?

I don't believe my eyes.

Do my eyes deceive me?

That's a sight for sore eyes.

44   Confirming that you are paying attention

I hear you.

I heard you.

I'm listening.

I'm still here.

I'm all ears.

Launching the Conversation

45   Starting an informal conversation

Guess what?

Have you heard the latest?

Have you heard?

Did you hear what happened?

Did you hear the news?

Did you get the scoop? (*informal*)
   the scoop = the most recent news

You'll never guess what I heard.

You'll never guess what I read online.

Guess what I just saw online.

Guess what I just found out.

You won't believe this.

You won't believe what Bill just told me.

Get a load of this. (*informal*)

    a load = a sampling

Get this. (*informal*)

Dig this. (*slang*)

    to dig = to understand

46   Inviting someone to talk

You got a minute?

Got a minute?

I need to talk.

Can we talk?

Can I talk to you?

May I have a word with you? (*formal*)

Let's talk.

Let's chew the fat. (*slang*)

Let's shoot the breeze. (*slang*)

47   Coming to the point of the matter

May I be frank?

Let me be perfectly clear.

Make no bones about it. (*idiomatic*)

    = *Do not make any bones of contention about this.*

Read my lips. (*informal*)

    = *Pay close attention to what I am saying.*

(To a make a) long story short. (*cliché*)

Let's call a spade a spade. (*cliché*)

Let me spell it out for you.

Here's the bottom line.

the bottom line = the summation; the final and major point

48 Requesting that the speaker get to the point

What's your point?

What's the point?

What's the upshot?

the upshot = the result

What's the bottom line?

the bottom line = the summation; the final and major point

What are you trying to say?

What are you trying to tell me?

Get to the point.

Get to the heart of the matter.

Cut to the chase. (*idiomatic*)

= Switch to the focal point of something.

49 Various conversational phrases

If I may.

= If I may interrupt.; If I may add some information.

Pardon my French.

= Pardon my use of vulgar words.

No pun intended.

= I intended to make no joke or play on words.

If you know what I mean.

= I assume you understand what I mean.

Know what I mean? (*informal*)

= Do you understand what I am saying?

You know what I'm saying?

= Do you understand what I am saying?

You know?

= Do you understand what I am saying?

Right?

    = Is that not so?

OK?

    = Is that not so?

50   Encouraging someone to speak plainly

Enough already. (*informal*)

Out with it! (*informal*)

    = Say it!; Speak out!

Don't mince words.

    to mince = to cut up or disguise

Spare (me) nothing.

Lay it on the line. (*informal*)

Tell it to me like a man. (*informal*)

Give it to me straight. (*informal*)

    straight = unadorned

Give it to me in plain English.

    plain English = simple and direct terms

Don't beat around the bush. (*idiomatic*)

Stop beating around the bush. (*idiomatic*)

Stop circumventing the issue.

Put your cards on the table. (*idiomatic*)

Stop speaking in circles.

What does that mean in English? (*informal*)

Cut the crap. (*mildly vulgar*)

    crap = dung = needless talk

51   Noting digressions in a conversation

That's beside the point.

That's beside the question.

That's not at issue.

That's not the issue.

That's irrelevant.

That has nothing to do with it.

That has nothing to do with what I'm talking about.

That's another story.

That's a whole 'nother story. (*folksy*)

That's a different ball of wax. (*idiomatic*)

    ball of wax = thing; matter

That's a different kettle of fish. (*idiomatic*)

    kettle of fish = thing; matter

That's another can of worms. (*idiomatic*)

    can of worms = set of problems

That's a horse of a different color. (*idiomatic*)

    a horse of a different color = a different kind of problem altogether

You're off on a tangent.

You're getting off the subject.

As you were saying . . .

Getting back to the point . . .

But I digress. (*formal*)

52 Repeating what you have said

Let me repeat myself.

Allow me to repeat myself. (*formal*)

At the risk of repeating myself . . .

As I've said . . .

As I am fond of saying . . .

To reiterate . . .

To repeat . . .

How many times do I have to tell you?

If I've told you once, I've told you a thousand times. (*cliché*)

If I've said it once, I've said it a million times. (*cliché*)

53 When someone is being repetitious

So you said.

Stop beating a dead horse.

    beating a dead horse = continuing to argue a point that has been won

Stop harping on that subject.

> *harping on = dwelling on; talking about*

You sound like a broken record. (*idiomatic*)

> *broken record = a grooved LP album with a scratch that makes the same track repeat endlessly*

Must you belabor the point?
All right, already.
We get the point, already.
We heard you, already.

54   Agreeing with a speaker

So it seems.
So it would seem.
Or so it would appear.
As it were.
So to speak.
In a manner of speaking.

55   Answers to "How did you find out?"

I heard it through the grapevine.

> *the grapevine = a chain of rumors*

I heard it on the grapevine.
A little bird told me. (*cliché*)
I have my sources.
I got it straight from the horse's mouth. (*idiomatic*)

> *from the horse's mouth = from the source*

It's common knowledge.
We live in a fishbowl. (*informal*)

> *= We are completely on display.; We are openly visible to everyone.*

Word travels fast. (*cliché*)
News travels fast. (*cliché*)
Bad news travels fast. (*cliché*)
None of your business. (*informal*)

Just never (you) mind.

We have our ways (of finding these things out). (*jocular*)

I plead the fifth. (*informal*)

I'm taking the fifth. (*informal*)

> *the fifth = the Fifth Amendment to the U.S. Constitution, which*
> *protects against self-incrimination*

I'm not one to kiss and tell. (*cliché*)

> *to kiss and tell = to do something secret and tell everyone about it*

Making Friends

56   Expressing friendship

We're very close.

We're the closest of friends.

We're the best of friends.

We're best friends.

We're pretty tight.

They're bosom buddies.

She's my best friend.

She's my closest friend.

She's a dear friend.

She's like a sister to me.

He's like the brother I never had.

We're like brothers.

You're like the brother I never had!

57   Commenting on the uniqueness of someone

He's one of a kind.

Sue's one of a kind.

What a character!

They don't make them like him anymore. (*cliché*)

After they made him, they broke the mold. (*cliché*)

58 Commenting on personal similarities

We're two of a kind.

They're two of a kind.

We're cut from the same cloth.

We're made from the same mold.

We're birds of a feather. (*cliché*)

We're like two peas in a pod.

59 Expressions used to make friends at a bar or café

May I join you?

Is this stool taken?

Is this seat taken?

Do you care if I join you?

Care if I join you?

Do you mind if I join you?

Mind if I join you?

Care to join us?

Can I buy you a drink?

Could I buy you a drink?

Could I get you something to drink?

What are you drinking?

Do you know who does this song?

    does = sings

Would you like to play darts?

Let's play pool.

    pool = billiards

Do you mind if I join you?

60 Inviting someone to dance

Care to dance?

Would you like to dance?

You want to dance? (*informal*)

Could I have the next dance?

May I have the next dance? (*formal*)

61   Approaching the opposite sex

That's a pretty outfit. (*male to female*)

That's a pretty dress. (*male to female*)

What's shaking? (*slang*)

    shaking = happening

Don't I know you from somewhere?

Didn't we go to high school together?

Haven't I seen you here before?

Do you come here often?

What's a nice girl like you doing in a place like this? (*male to female, cliché*)

Do you have a smoke?

    a smoke = a cigarette

Do you have a light?

    a light = a match or cigarette lighter

Do you have a cigarette?

Do you have change for the cigarette machine?

Would you like to go somewhere quieter?

Are you going my way?

Going my way? (*cliché*)

Could I give you a lift?

    a lift = a ride

Need a lift?

Where have you been keeping yourself?

Where have you been all my life? (*cliché*)

62   Asking someone for a date

Are you free Saturday evening?

Are you free Saturday night?

Are you busy on the 15th?

What are you up to this weekend?

What are you doing next weekend?

Would you like to go to dinner?

Would you like to go out to dinner with me?

I was wondering if you'd like to go out.

I was wondering if you'd like to see a movie.

If you're not doing anything, would you like to go to a party with me?

If you don't have other plans, would you like to go dancing?

63   Turning someone down

Not if you were the last man on earth.

I'm not interested.

I'm seeing someone else.

I have other plans.

I've got something going on.

Something suddenly came up.

I have to wash my hair.

My calendar is full.

You're not my type.

Not if you were the last man on earth. (*rude*)

You must be joking. (*rude*)

I don't feel up to it.

I have a headache.

Please. (*with a disgusted tone of voice*)

64   Bringing a conversation to an end

Let's call it a day.

Let's call it a night.

Let's call it quits.

> = *Let's quit (and leave).*

Let's get out of here.

Let's get going.

Let's go.

We should be on our way.

Let's bid our farewell. (*formal*)

Let's say our good-byes. (*formal*)

65   Expressing support for someone

I'll stand by you.
I'm standing behind you.
I am 100 percent behind you.
I'm with you.
I'm on your side.
I've got your back. (*informal*)
You've got my support.
You've got my backing.
You've got my vote.
You can count on me.
You can lean on me.
You can trust me.
You can put your trust in me.
You can put your faith in me.

66   Offering help to someone

If there's anything I can do to help, please let me know.
Let me know if there's anything I can do.
I'm here if you need me.
I'm here for you.
If you need me, call.
I'll always be there for you.
I'll go to bat for you.
> *to go to bat for you = to support you*

I'll take the rap. (*slang*)
> *the rap = the blame*

67   Expressing trust in someone

I have faith in you.
I have the utmost faith in you.

I have complete faith in you.
I trust you completely.
I trust you implicitly.
I have faith in you.
I have confidence in you.

68   Expressing encouragement

Go on; you can do it!

Just one more.

Just a little harder.

Hang in there.

Stick with it.

Stay at it.

Go for it.

Give it a try.

Give it a shot.

> *a shot = a try*

Give it your best shot.

Give it your best.

Keep at it.

Keep your nose to the grindstone. (*idiomatic*)

> *= Keep bent over your work. = Keep working hard.*

Hang in there. (*informal*)

Hang tough. (*slang*)

Stick it out. (*informal*)

69   Encouraging someone to try something

Have a go at it.

> *a go = a try*

Take a shot at it. (*informal*)

> *a shot = a try*

Take a stab at it. (*informal*)

> *a stab = a try*

Take a crack at it. (*informal*)

    a crack = a try

Have a crack at it.

Take a whack at it. (*informal*)

    a whack = a try

Come on. (*informal*)

It won't hurt you to try it.

Everybody's doing it.

Everyone else is doing it.

It's all the rage.

    the rage = the current fad

Try your luck.

See what you can do.

Nothing ventured, nothing gained. (*cliché*)

Go on.

Get going.

Get going already.

Get moving.

No pain, no gain. (*cliché*)

Get a move on. (*informal*)

Get cracking. (*slang*)

Get on the stick. (*slang*)

Get the lead out. (*slang*)

Get off your ass. (*mildly vulgar*)

70   Encouraging someone to stop stalling and do something

Let's see some action. (*informal*)

It's now or never.

Take no prisoners! (*informal*)

Fish or cut bait! (*idiomatic*)

Knock yourself out. (*idiomatic*)

    = *Try really hard.; Work as hard as you can.*

Go for broke. (*informal*)

    = *Risk everything.*

I expect to see some results soon.

Are you just going to stand there all day?

Are you just going to sit there?

Aren't you going to do anything?

Are you just going to sit there like a bump on a log? (*informal*)

   a bump on a log = a motionless object

You're letting the world pass you by.

71   Expressing dissatisfaction with someone's efforts

That won't do.

That won't do it.

That doesn't cut it. (*idiomatic*)

   to cut it = to do what is needed

That doesn't cut the mustard. (*idiomatic*)

   to cut the mustard = to measure up to expectations

That doesn't make the grade.

   to make the grade = to qualify

Is that it?

It's not up to snuff.

Is that all?

You call that finished?

Once more with feeling. (*cliché*)

That doesn't cut the mustard.

72   Asking someone to wait

Wait.

Wait a moment.

Wait a minute.

Wait a sec(ond).

Wait one moment.

Wait one minute.

Wait one sec(ond).

Wait it out.

Wait your turn.

Just a moment.

Just a minute.

Just a sec(ond).

Just one moment.

Just one minute.

Just one sec(ond).

Hold your horses. (*idiomatic*)

    = *Wait a bit.*

Keep your pants on. (*informal*)

    = *Wait a bit.*

Keep your shirt on. (*informal*)

    = *Wait a bit.*

73   Encouraging someone to be patient and take things slowly

Take things as they come.

Take it as it comes.

Take it one day at a time.

Take things one day at a time.

Take one day at a time.

Time will tell. (*cliché*)

    = *We will know more in time.*

Rome wasn't built in a day. (*cliché*)

    = *Big projects require a lot of time.*

A watched pot never boils. (*cliché*)

    = *Paying constant attention to something you are waiting for will make the wait seem endless.*

Good things come to him who waits. (*cliché*)

One step at a time.

One day at a time.

Good things come to those who wait. (*cliché*)

Patience is a virtue. (*cliché*)

In good time.

All in good time.

Everything in its time.

There's a time for everything.

It will work out in the end.

Everything will come together.

Everything will fall together.

Everything will fall into place.

In the long run, everything
    will be OK. (*informal*)

In the long haul, it will all
    work out.

Everything will work itself out.

I am confident it will all
    work out.

It ain't over till it's over. (*informal*)

It ain't over till the fat lady
    sings. (*cliché*)

    = *The opera is not over until the overweight opera singer has done
        her solo.* = *The event will not conclude until everything that was
        planned to happen has happened.*

74   Encouraging someone to be prudent—clichés

Don't jump the gun.

    *to jump the gun = to start a race before the starting gun is fired =
        to do something too early*

Don't go off half-cocked.

    half-cocked = ill-prepared

Don't go chomping at the bit.

    chomp = to bite (as with an eager horse)

Don't put the cart before the horse.

Don't count your chickens before they hatch.

    = *Don't base your plans on something that hasn't developed yet.*

Don't cross that bridge till you come to it.

    = *We will deal with that when the time comes.*

We'll cross that bridge when we come to it.

Don't get ahead of yourself.

75   Giving advice to someone whose life is too busy

You can't please everybody. (*cliché*)
You can't be all things to all people. (*cliché*)
You've got your fingers in too many pies. (*idiomatic*)
You've got your irons in too many fires. (*idiomatic*)
You're burning the candle at both ends. (*cliché*)
You're taking too many things on.
You're taking on too much.
You're doing too much.
You're trying to do too much.
You're overcommitted.
You're overdoing it.
You're carrying the world on your shoulders.
You need to set your priorities.

76   Giving instructions to someone you've lent something to

Take care of it.
Take good care of it.
I'm trusting you to take good care of it.
Keep an eye on it.
Guard it with your life.
Don't let it out of your sight.
I want this back.
I want it back in one piece.
    in one piece = unbroken; unharmed
Bring it back in one piece.

77   Introducing a secret

Just between you and me . . .
Just between you, me, and the lamppost . . .
This is between you, me, and the bedpost.
This is between you, me, and the four walls.
I'm telling you this in confidence.

I'm telling you this in strict confidence.

I'm telling you this in strictest confidence.

Can you keep a secret?

Don't repeat this, but . . .

Don't let this get around, but . . .

Could you keep a secret?

Confidentially . . .

78   Instructions about keeping a secret

Better keep quiet about it.

Better keep still about it.

Keep it to yourself.

Don't breathe a word of this to anyone.

Don't breathe a word of it.

Don't let it out of this room.

    it = the secret

Don't let this go any further.

Don't tell a soul.

    a soul = a person

Mum's the word.

    mum = a word referring to a closed mouth

It's on the QT. (*slang*)

    QT = quiet

Play dumb.

This is top secret.

This is for your eyes only.

This is for your ears only.

Don't say I told you.

Don't say who told you.

This is off the record.

    off the record = not to be reported or quoted

This is not for the record.

This is not to be quoted.

This is not for public knowledge.

This is not public knowledge.

This is not for publication.

79 Promising to keep a secret

I won't tell a soul.

   a soul = a person

My lips are sealed. (*cliché*)

It won't leave this room.

Wild horses couldn't drag it out of me. (*cliché*)

I'll take it to my grave.

   = I'll die without telling the secret to anyone.

80 Forgetfulness

Where was I?

   = What was I saying?

What was I saying?

What were we talking about?

I don't remember.

I have a mind like a sieve.

   a sieve = a strainer or colander

I'm a little absentminded.

   absentminded = forgetful

I'd lose my head if it weren't attached. (*informal*)

I've lost my train of thought.

   train of thought = sequence of thoughts

It's at the tip of my tongue.

   = It is about ready to be said.

It's on the tip of my tongue.

It's slipped my mind.

The thought escapes me.

It's left my head.

What was your name again?

What did you just say?

It went in one ear and out the other. (*cliché*)

Are we supposed to be someplace right now?

81 When you are in trouble

I'm in trouble.

I'm in big trouble.

I'm in deep trouble.

I'm in deep.

I'm in over my head.

I'm in way over my head.

I'm behind the eight ball. (*idiomatic*)
> = *I'm in trouble with someone.*

My ass is in a sling. (*mildly vulgar*)
> *in a sling = injured = at risk*

My ass is on the line. (*mildly vulgar*)
> *on the line = at risk*

My neck is on the line.

My job is on the line.

My reputation is on the line.

My reputation is at stake.
> *at stake = at risk*

82 When someone is in trouble

Your goose is cooked. (*idiomatic*)
> = *You are in trouble.*

You've really screwed up. (*informal*)

You've done it now.

Now you've done it.

You've really done it this time.

You're in for it.

You're gonna get it. (*informal*)

How could you do something so stupid?

What kind of mess did you get yourself into?

That's another fine mess you've gotten us into. (*informal*)

How are you going to dig yourself out of this one?

How are you going to get out of this one?

You've made your bed; now lie in it.

    = *You have created this situation, so you must endure it.*

You're up the creek without a paddle. (*informal*)

You're up a creek. (*informal*)

You're up the creek. (*informal*)

83   When you are out of money

I'm broke.

    broke = without any money

I'm dead broke.

I'm flat broke.

I'm flatter than a pancake. (*informal*)

    flatter than a pancake = as flat broke as is possible

I don't have a dollar to my name.

    to my name = in my ownership

I'm dead broke!

I don't have a penny to my name.

I don't have a cent to my name.

I don't have a red cent. (*informal*)

    red cent = a copper penny

I'm busted. (*slang*)

    busted = without any money

I'm as poor as a church mouse. (*idiomatic*)

My pockets are empty.

I have empty pockets.

All I have is the shirt on my back.

    the shirt on my back = the clothes that you see me in

I've got nothing but the shirt on my back.

All I have is my good name.

    my good name = my reputation

I don't know where my next meal is coming from.

My savings are wiped out.

I've lost everything.

I'm bankrupt.

84   When someone is in debt

I'm in the red.

> red = red ink = indebtedness

She's in over her head (in debt). (*idiomatic*)

I'm up to my ears in debt. (*idiomatic*)

Bill's writing rubber checks.

> a rubber check = a bad check (that bounces back from the bank
> because there is no money to pay it)

I'm borrowing from Peter to pay Paul. (*idiomatic*)

I'm robbing Peter to pay Paul. (*idiomatic*)

85   Expressing stress or anxiety

I'm going nuts. (*slang*)

> nuts = crazy

I'm going crazy.

I'm losing my mind.

I'm losing my marbles. (*informal*)

> losing my marbles = losing my intellect

I'm freaking out. (*slang*)

I'm spazzing out. (*slang*)

I'm mad at the world.

I need a break.

I need some sleep.

I'm going to explode.

My head is going to explode.

Everything is getting on my nerves.

I can't take it anymore.

I can't take another problem.

I can't deal with this anymore.

I'm on pins and needles. (*idiomatic*)
 on pins and needles = in anxious anticipation

I'm on tenterhooks.
 tenterhooks = a type of sharp nail used for fastening fabric

I'm a bundle of nerves.

I've got butterflies in my stomach. (*idiomatic*)
 = My stomach is feeling like it is fluttering.

I'm coming apart at the seams.

I'm falling apart at the seams.

86 When you are overworked and doing too much

I'm burning the candle at both ends. (*cliché*)
I scarcely have time to breathe.
I have no time to call my own.

87 When someone is anxious and under stress

Calm down.
Simmer down.
Control yourself. (*informal*)
Don't go into hysterics.
Don't be such a worrywart.
 a worrywart = a person who worries a lot
Don't worry yourself sick.
Don't lose sleep over it.
Don't let it get to you.
Don't trouble yourself.
You'll send yourself to an early grave.
 an early grave = an early death

88 Encouraging someone not to be offended—informal

Don't get all bent out of shape!
Don't get your nose out of joint!

Don't be so sensitive!
Learn to roll with the punches.
I didn't mean any harm.

89 Encouraging someone not to be excited

Pull yourself together.
Don't get excited.
Don't get all excited.
Don't get all worked up.
Don't blow your stack. (*slang*)
    to blow your stack = to lose your
       temper; to go crazy

Don't lose your cool. (*slang*)
Don't blow your cool. (*slang*)
Don't blow a gasket. (*slang*)
Don't go into hysterics.
Don't go into hysterics on me.
Don't fly off the handle.
Don't pop your cork. (*slang*)
    to pop your cork = to go crazy

Don't work yourself into a tizzy. (*informal*)
    a tizzy = a dizzy, confused state

Don't run around like a chicken with its head cut off. (*informal*)
Restrain yourself.
Would you restrain yourself?
Get a grip (on yourself). (*informal*)
Would you get a grip? (*informal*)

90 Encouraging someone to relax

Mellow out. (*slang*)
    = *Adopt a calm attitude.*
Chill out. (*slang*)
Chill. (*slang*)
Keep cool. (*slang*)

Cool it. (*slang*)

Cool your jets. (*slang*)

Cool off. (*informal*)

Cool down. (*informal*)

Slow down.

Simmer down.

Calm down.

Be calm.

Calm yourself.

Relax.

Deal with it. (*informal*)

Hold your horses. (*cliché*)

Keep your shirt on. (*informal*)

Keep your pants on. (*informal*)

Take a deep breath.

Take it easy.

Take it slow.

Take a tranquilizer! (*informal*)

Take a pill! (*informal*)

91   Encouraging someone to be less aggressive—informal

Don't have a cow!

Don't have a conniption fit.

Don't throw a fit.

Don't have a fit.

Give it a break.

Give it a rest.

You got ants in your pants?

92   When someone is cold and unfeeling—informal

You're as cold as ice.

You're a cold fish.

You're cold-blooded.

You've got a heart of stone.

You've got no heart.
You're heartless.
You're thick-skinned.
Have you no qualms?
Have you no scruples?
Have you no conscience?
Have you no thought for anyone but yourself?
Think before you speak.
Think before you act.
Try putting yourself in my shoes.
 = *Think what it is like to be in my situation.*

93   What to say to a smoker

This is a nonsmoking area.
This is a nonsmoking building.
You'll have to step outside.
Please observe the no-smoking
    signs. (*formal*)
Can you put that out?
Please put that out.
I'm sorry, you'll have to put that out.
I'm sorry, the smoke is bothering me.
Have you ever thought of quitting?
It's your funeral. (*informal*)
You smoke like a chimney. (*informal*)

94   A smoker's response to a nonsmoker's complaint

Mind your own business.
Go to a nonsmoking area.
I can't quit.
I tried quitting.
I have no intention of quitting.
Sorry.

Got a match?
You got a lighter?
Can I bum a light?
    to bum = to beg
Can I bum a cigarette off you?
Can I have a drag?
    a drag = a puff of smoke
Where is the smoking room?
Where can you smoke around here?
Do you mind if I smoke?

Disputes

96 **Criticism of someone with whom you disagree**

You're clueless. (*informal*)
You're without a clue. (*informal*)
You wouldn't know the truth if it jumped up and bit you on the
    nose. (*jocular*)
She doesn't know nothing. (*informal*)
You don't know beans. (*informal*)
You don't know up from down. (*informal*)
You don't know which end is up. (*informal*)
You don't know your ass from your elbow. (*vulgar*)
You don't know your ass from a hole in the ground. (*vulgar*)
You don't know quality from a hole in the ground. (*informal*)
    quality = art, value, truth, engines, etc.

Don't you know anything?
How can you be so stupid? (*informal*)
Get your head out of the sand. (*idiomatic*)
That ain't the way I heard it. (*folksy*)

That's not what I heard.
Let me set you straight.

97 Calling someone crazy

You're off your rocker. (*informal*)
You're out of your mind. (*informal*)
He's two bricks shy of a load. (*slang*)
You're out of your tree. (*slang*)
You're out of your head. (*informal*)
She's out of her skull. (*informal*)
You've lost your marbles. (*informal*)
You're crazy. (*informal*)
You're nuts. (*informal*)
They can't be serious.
You're a few cards shy of a full deck. (*idiomatic*)
You're a few cards short of a deck. (*idiomatic*)
You aren't playing with a full deck. (*idiomatic*)
You're one sandwich short of a picnic. (*idiomatic*)
Your front porch light is out.
You've gone over the edge.
You've gone off the deep end.
You're nutty as a fruitcake. (*cliché*)

98 Questioning someone's sanity

Are you crazy?
Is he nuts? (*slang*)
    nuts = crazy
Are you psychotic, or what?
Are you out of your mind?
Are you out of your head?
Are you out of your gourd? (*informal*)
    gourd = head
Are you out of your skull? (*informal*)
Are you out of your tree? (*slang*)

Are you out of it?

Have you gone crazy?

Have you gone insane?

Have you gone mad?

Have you gone stark raving mad?

Have you gone loco? (*informal*)
  loco (Spanish) = crazy

Have you gone plumb loco? (*informal*)
  plumb loco = completely crazy

Have you lost your mind?

Have you lost your senses?

Have you lost your marbles?

Have you wigged out? (*slang*)

Have you completely flipped out? (*slang*)

Have you flipped your lid? (*slang*)

Have you completely lost it? (*informal*)

Have you completely lost touch with reality?

Have you taken leave of your senses?

Do you have a screw loose? (*slang*)

What planet are you from?

Do you have rocks in your head? (*informal*)

Do you have bats in your belfry? (*slang*)

Are there bats in your belfry? (*slang*)

Are you playing with a full deck? (*slang*)

99   Asking about the alertness of someone

Hello? (*informal*)

What are you thinking?

What's your deal? (*informal*)

What's your problem? (*informal*)

What ([kind of] drugs) are you on? (*informal*)

What have you been smoking? (*informal*)

Where's your head? (*informal*)

What's with you? (*informal*)

Are you serious?

What planet are you on? (*informal*)

Earth to Bill. (*informal*)

100 Encouraging someone to be more sensible

Get a life! (*informal*)

Get real!

Snap out of it.

Get with the program. (*informal*)

Come back to earth. (*informal*)

101 Asking in disbelief or disagreement

Are you bullshitting me?

Truly?

Really?

For real? (*informal*)

No kidding?

No fooling? (*informal*)

No lie? (*informal*)

No way! (*informal*)

Are you serious?

Are you for real? (*informal*)

Are you pulling my leg?

Are you bullshitting me? (*mildly vulgar*)

You're not making this up, are you?

You're making this up, aren't you?

You're not trying to pull one over on me, are you?

102 When someone says something outrageous

Unbelievable!

Get out of town!

You're kidding!

You've got to be kidding!

You've got to be kidding me!

Stop it! (*informal*)

Come on! (*informal*)
Get out of here! (*informal*)
I can't believe it!
Do you expect me to believe that?
That blows my mind. (*informal*)

Discussion and Resolution

103 Asking for an explanation

What do you mean?
What are you saying?
What are you trying to get at?
What are you getting at?
Do you mean to tell me?
What's the bottom line?
This all boils down to what? (*idiomatic*)
How so?
So what's the upshot?
What's the point?

104 Encouraging an explanation

I didn't get that.
I didn't hear you.
Cut to the chase. (*idiomatic*)

105 When you do not understand someone

I don't see what you're getting at.
I don't get it.
I don't follow you.
I don't follow.

I'm not sure I follow.

I'm not sure I get your point.

I'm not sure I know what you mean.

106 When someone does not understand you

That's not what I meant.

That's not what I said.

I didn't mean that.

I didn't say that.

I said no such thing.

I didn't mean to give you that impression.

I didn't mean to imply that.

107 Criticizing someone's misunderstanding

Listen to me.

Open your ears. (*informal*)

Get the wax out of your ears. (*informal*)

You're not listening to what I'm saying.

You're only hearing what you want to hear.

You're missing the point.

That's not my point.

That's not the point I'm trying
    to make.

You've got it wrong.

You've got it all wrong.

You've got me wrong.

You've twisted my words.

You're putting words in my mouth.

You're quoting me out of context.

You're taking it out of context.

You're blowing it out of proportion.

You're blowing this all out
    of proportion.

108   Attempting to put an end to a misunderstanding

Let me rephrase that.
Let me clarify that.
Allow me to clarify.
Let me make myself clear.
Let me make myself perfectly clear.

109   Encouraging someone to believe you

Honest.
Honestly.
Truly.
True.
That's the truth.
That's the honest truth.
That's the honest-to-goodness truth.
Honest to goodness.
That's the truth, the whole truth, and nothing but the truth.
Cross my heart and hope to die. (*juvenile*)
Would I lie?
Would I lie to you?
Why would I lie?
I swear.
I swear to you.
I swear on a stack of Bibles. (*mild oath*)
I swear on my mother's grave. (*informal*)
I swear to God. (*mild oath*)
May God strike me down if I am not telling you the truth. (*mild oath*)
That's the gospel truth. (*informal*)

110   Asking to be trusted

Take my word for it.
You have my word.

You have my word on this.
I give you my word.
I give you my word of honor.
On my honor.
Scout's honor. (*juvenile*)
You can count on it.
You can bank on it.
You can take it to the bank.
You better believe it.
You had better believe it.
Believe you me.
Trust me.
Don't be such a doubting Thomas.

111   Stating that something is settled

It's cinched.
It's locked up.
It's sewn up.
It's a sure thing.
It's for sure.
It's certain.
It's in the bag.
It's a done deal.
It's as good as done.
Nothing can go wrong.
What can go wrong?
All's well that ends well. (*cliché*)
That's that.
What's to go wrong?
It's going to happen.
There's no doubt in my mind.
There's not a doubt in my mind.

112   Claiming that something is easy to understand

It's as plain as day.
It's as clear as day.
It's as plain as the nose on your face. (*jocular*)
Do I need to paint you a picture? (*informal*)
Must I paint you a picture? (*informal*)
That goes without saying.
Any fool can see it. (*informal*)

113   Showing disbelief

I find that hard to believe.
Unbelievable.
I find that hard to swallow.
I'll take that with a grain of salt. (*cliché*)
I remain skeptical.
I'll believe it when I see it.
You can't fool me.
You can't pull the wool over my eyes.
I wasn't born yesterday.

114   Expressing ignorance

Dunno. (*informal*)
I don't know.
I don't know and I don't care.
I don't have a clue.
I haven't a clue.
I'm clueless.
I don't have the faintest idea.
I haven't the faintest idea.
I haven't the vaguest notion.
I don't have the foggiest notion.
Haven't the foggiest.
Beats me. (*informal*)

Beats the heck out of me. (*informal*)
Beats the hell out of me. (*mildly vulgar*)
Got me beat. (*informal*)
You got me (there).
Got me stumped. (*informal*)
Got me.
How would I know?
How should I know?
How the hell should I know? (*mildly vulgar*)
Like I would know. (*informal*)
Like I would know? (*informal*)
I give up. (*informal*)
Search me. (*informal*)
Who knows?
Lord knows. (*mild oath*)
God only knows. (*mild oath*)

115   **Expressing reluctance**

I'm afraid not.
'Fraid not.
I'm afraid so.
'Fraid so.
If I must. (*formal*)
Well, if I have to.
Well, if you insist.
Well, if you really think so.
Well, if you really want me to.
I guess I have no choice in the matter.
It doesn't sound like I have a choice.
We've got no choice.
We have no alternative.
There's no alternative.
I'd rather not.
I'd rather die.
I'd sooner die.

Never in a thousand years.
Not in a million years.
Over my dead body. (*informal*)

116   Making the best of a bad situation

That's life.
That's the way life is.
That's how it goes.
That's the way it goes.
That's the way the ball bounces. (*cliché*)
That's the way the cookie crumbles. (*cliché*)
Things could be worse.
It's not as bad as all that.
Look on the bright(er) side. (*cliché*)
Make the best of it.
Half a loaf is better than none. (*cliché*)
It's always darkest before dawn. (*cliché*)
Every cloud has a silver lining. (*cliché*)
When life hands you lemons, make lemonade. (*cliché*)
It's the best we can do under the circumstances.
I wish we could do more.
You did the best you could.
You did the best that could be expected.
You get an A for effort.
The important thing is that you tried.
Winning isn't everything. (*cliché*)
You can't win them all. (*cliché*)
It's not whether you win or lose, it's how you play the game. (*cliché*)
You made a noble effort.
Truth is stranger than fiction. (*cliché*)
It was just one of those things. (*cliché*)
(Don't ask why;) it just is.
Why ask why? (*informal*)
Who am I to question?
It's for the best. (*cliché*)

It's all for the best. (*cliché*)

When God closes a door, He opens a window. (*cliché*)

Don't let it get you down.

Keep your chin up! (*cliché*)

Chin up!

Cheer up!

Keep a stiff upper lip. (*cliché*)

Grin and bear it. (*cliché*)

Grit your teeth. (*cliché*)

Take it in stride. (*cliché*)

Roll with the punches. (*cliché*)

Accept your fate.

You've made your bed; now lie in it. (*cliché*)

If at first you don't succeed, try, try again. (*cliché*)

The important thing is to learn from your mistakes.

The third time's the charm. (*cliché*)

I'm between a rock and a hard place. (*cliché*)

I'm between the devil and the deep blue sea. (*cliché*)

I'm damned if I do and damned if I don't. (*mildly vulgar*)

You're damned if you do and damned if you don't. (*mildly vulgar*)

117   Blaming something on fate or destiny

It was destiny.

It was destined to happen.

It's your fate.

It was fated to happen.

It's fate.

It's in the cards.

It's in the stars.

It's the cruel hand of fate.

That's karma.

It's God's will.

It's all in God's plan.

It was meant to be.

Que sera, sera. (*Spanish*)

   = *Whatever will be, will be.*

What will be, will be.

Whatever will be, will be.

Don't fight it.

You can't fight it.

You can't fight City Hall.

There's nothing you can do about it.

You have to play the hand life deals you.

You've got to play the hand you're dealt.

118   Knowing something after the fact

I should have known.

I should have known better.

If I (only) knew then what I know now . . .

If I (just) knew then what I know now . . .

If I'd known then what I know now . . .

If only I could turn back the hands of time.

If I could only turn back the clock.

It's easy to be wise after the event.

That's easy to say in hindsight.

Hindsight is 20/20.

   20/20 = good vision in each eye at twenty feet = hindsight

119   Expressing indifference

I don't care.

I couldn't care less.

I could care less. (*informal*)

I don't give a damn. (*mildly vulgar*)

Like I give a damn. (*mildly vulgar*)

It doesn't matter to me.

Really doesn't matter to me.

Makes no difference to me.

Makes me no difference. (*informal*)

Makes me no nevermind. (*folksy*)

Makes no nevermind to me. (*folksy*)

Either way.

Whichever.

Whatever.

Six of one, half (a) dozen of the other. (*informal*)

Up to you.

Whatever you prefer.

It's not important.

I guess so.

I guess.

POLITE ENCOUNTERS

Prefaces

120   A preface to asking a question

Excuse me . . .

Pardon me . . .

Excuse me for asking . . .

If you don't mind my asking . . .

It's none of my business, but . . .

121   A preface to making a statement—formal

If I may say so . . .

If I may be so bold . . .

If it's okay with you . . .

If it pleases you . . .

Please be advised that . . .

For your information . . .

It is a pleasure to inform you that . . .
We regret to inform you that . . .
As you are aware . . .
As you are no doubt aware . . .
As you know . . .
As you might know . . .
As you may already know . . .

122   A preface to making a statement—informal

(To make a) long story short . . .
What I would like to say is . . .
But I just wanted to say . . .
By the way . . .
If you ask me . . .
Not that it's any of my business . . .

123   A preface to making a statement—very polite

As you requested . . .
For your convenience . . .
We apologize for the inconvenience . . .
With your safety in mind . . .
With your comfort in mind . . .

Communication Barriers

124   Asking if someone speaks a particular language

Do you speak French?
    French = Spanish, German, Russian, Italian, etc.
Do you know any French?
Do you speak any French?

125   When you do not speak a particular language

I'm sorry. I don't understand.
I'm sorry. I don't speak French.
   French = Spanish, German, Russian, Italian, etc.
I'm sorry. My French isn't very good.
I only speak a little French.

126   When you do not understand what was said

Pardon me?
Excuse me?
Again, (please).
I'm sorry?
I'm sorry. I missed that.
   missed that = failed to hear what was said
I didn't quite get that.
   to get that = to hear or understand what was said
What did you say?
I'm sorry. What?
What?
What was that?
Come again. (*folksy*)
Huh? (informal or rude)
Could you please repeat yourself?
Could you please repeat that?

127   When you do not understand what a foreign visitor has said

I don't understand you.
I can't understand you.
I can't hear you.
Please speak more slowly.
Could you please speak slower?
Could you please speak louder?
Could you write it down, please?

Please write it out.
Could you spell that?

Telling Time

128   Asking the time of day

What time is it?
Could you tell me what time it is?
Could you please tell me the time?
Could you give me the time?
Do you know what time it is?
Do you know the time?
Do you happen to have the time?
Do you have the correct time?
Do you have the time?
Could I bother you for the time?

Do you happen to have the time?

129   The time is 12:00 o'clock

It's twelve noon.
It's noon.
It's twelve midnight.
It's midnight.

130   The time is on the hour

It's three.
It's three o'clock.
It's three o'clock sharp.
It's three o'clock on the dot.
It's three o'clock on the nose. (*informal*)
It's exactly three o'clock.

131   **The time is approximate**

It's almost three.
It's not quite three.
It's just after three.

It's ten past three.

132   **The time is ten minutes past the hour**

It's ten after three.
It's ten after.
It's ten minutes after three.
It's ten past three.
It's ten past.

133   **The time is fifteen or thirty minutes past the hour**

It's three fifteen.
It's a quarter past three.
It's three thirty.
It's half past three.
It's half past.

134   **The time is forty minutes past the hour**

It's three forty.
It's twenty of four.
It's twenty to four.
It's twenty till four.
It's twenty minutes till four.

135   **The time is forty-five minutes past the hour**

It's three forty-five.
It's quarter to four.
It's a quarter of four.
It's quarter to.

It's a quarter of.
It's a quarter till.
It's a quarter till four.

136 The time is fifty minutes past the hour

It's ten minutes to four.
It's ten to four.
It's ten to.
It's ten of.
It's ten till.

137 When a timepiece is not accurate

Is this clock right?
I think my watch needs a new battery.
This clock is fast.
This clock is slow.
My watch is running fast.
My watch has been running slow.

I think my watch needs a new battery!

General Pleasantries

138 When your moving about may bother someone

Excuse me.
Pardon me.
Coming through.
I beg your pardon.
Could I get by, please?
Watch your feet!

139   Offering to let someone enter in front of you

Be my guest.

After you.
Ladies first.
You first.
Age before beauty. (*jocular cliché*)
Be my guest.

140   Apologizing to someone you have bothered

I'm sorry.
Forgive me.
Sorry to be a bother.
Sorry to be a pest.
Sorry for the inconvenience.
Please forgive the inconvenience.

141   Returning someone's good wishes

Same to you.
Likewise.
Likewise, I'm sure. (*cliché*)
Thank you.

142   Agreeing to something—polite

Of course.
Be happy to.
Fine.
Great.
Super. (*slang*)

143   Explaining that you will attend to someone soon

I'll be there in just a moment.
Be there in a minute.

I'll be right with you.
I'll be with you in a moment.

144   Asking for permission to leave a place—polite

Could I be excused?
May I be excused?
Might I be excused? (*formal*)

145   Saying good-bye—polite

Good afternoon.
Good evening.
Good morning.
Good day.
Good night.
Have a nice day.
Good-bye.
Bye.
Bye-bye.
Farewell.
Good-bye until later.
Good-bye until next time.
Good-bye for now.

146   Saying good-bye—informal

So long.
Ta-ta.
Farewell.
Cheerio.
See you later.
See you later, alligator. (*slang*)
Later, gator. (*slang*)

Later.

I'll try to catch you later.

I'll catch you later.

Catch you later.

See you.

See ya.

See you around.

Take care.

Business Pleasantries

147   Announcing your arrival for an appointment

Mr. Smith to see Dr. Jones.

I'm here to see Mrs. Hodges.

Could you please tell Mr. Smith I'm here?

I have an appointment with Mrs. Jones.

148   Being assertive—polite

I'd like my check now, please.

I'd like my payment now, please.

No, I don't think so.

     = *I totally reject your assertion.*

Excuse me?

     = *Did you really say what I think you said?*

May I have your name, please?

I'd like to speak to the manager.

I'd like to speak to your supervisor.

I intend to stand my ground.

I'm not leaving until I'm satisfied.

149   Sincere apologies

Sorry.

So sorry.

I'm (so) very sorry.

I'm (so) sorry.

I'm really sorry.

I'm terribly sorry.

I'm sincerely sorry.

I apologize.

My apologies. (*formal*)

My sincere apologies. (*formal*)

You have my sincere apology. (*formal*)

Please accept my apology.

Please accept my apologies.

Please accept my heartfelt apology.

I offer my most sincere apology. (*formal*)

150   Offering a very polite apology

You cannot believe how sorry I am.

Words cannot describe how sorry I am.

I am just mortified.

Please send me the bill, and I'll take care of it.

151   Accepting the blame for something

It's my fault.

It's all my fault.

I'm fully responsible.

I take full responsibility.

I take the blame.

I blame no one but myself.

Mea culpa. (*Latin*)

   = *I am guilty.*

Maxima culpa. (*Latin*)

   = *I am completely guilty.*

152 Admitting your errors

Sorry. I shouldn't have said that.

My mistake.

I shouldn't have said that.

I shouldn't have done that.

I should have asked you firs[t]

I didn't mean it.

I honestly didn't mean it.

I didn't mean it, honest.

I didn't mean to do it.

I didn't mean to do that.

I didn't mean to say that.

I didn't mean it that way.

I didn't intend it that way.

I don't know how that could have happened.

153 Promising never to repeat a particular mistake

It won't happen again.

It will never happen again.

I'll see (to it) that it never happens again.

I won't do it again.

154 Offering to make amends

How can I make it up to you?

How can I ever make it up to you?

Is there anything I can do (to make it up to you)?

I promise I'll make it up to you.

Please forgive me.
Can you forgive me?
Can you ever forgive me?
Can you find it in your heart to forgive me?
How can you ever forgive me?
I ask your forgiveness.
I beg your forgiveness. (*formal*)
I throw myself upon your mercy. (*formal*)
I ask for your mercy. (*formal*)

Forgiving

156   Simple forgiveness

I forgive you.
You're forgiven.
All is forgiven.
That's all right.
It's okay. (*informal*)
That's okay. (*informal*)
Don't worry about it.
Think on it no more. (*formal*)
Think of it no more. (*formal*)
Think no more of it. (*formal*)
Don't give it another thought.
To err is human, to forgive divine. (*cliché*)

157   Forgiveness—informal

Forget it.
Forget about it.
Forgive and forget.

Don't worry about it.
Write it off.
I'll let you off this time.
I'll let it slide this time.
I'll give you another chance.
I'll turn the other cheek.
I won't hold it against you.

158   Encouraging someone to end a dispute

Let's drop the subject.
Let's bury the hatchet. (*idiomatic*)
Let's bring this matter to a close.
It's time to kiss and make up. (*cliché*)

Showing Gratitude

159   Saying "thank you"—formal

Thank you.
Thank you very much.
Thank you so much.
Thank you for your help.
Thank you for all you've done.
Thank you for everything.
You have my thanks.
You have my gratitude.
I'm deeply grateful.
I'm in your debt.
I'm indebted to you.
Thanks ever so much.
Thanks very much.

160 Saying "thank you"—informal

Thanks.

Thanks much.

Thanks for everything.

Thanks so much.

Thanks a lot.

Thanks a million.

Thanks a bunch.

Thanks a bundle.

Thanks heaps.

I owe you one.

I owe you big.

I owe you big-time.

Returning Thanks

161 Acknowledging someone's thanks—formal

You're welcome.

You're most welcome.

You're entirely welcome.

My pleasure.

It was my pleasure.

The pleasure was mine.

The pleasure was all mine.

The pleasure was entirely mine.

162 Acknowledging someone's thanks—informal

It was nothing.

Don't mention it.

No problem.

No sweat. (*slang*)

Any time.
No trouble.
No skin off my nose.
No skin off my teeth.
No skin off my back.

Special Occasions

163 Seeing a new baby

Oh, isn't he cute!
Isn't he the sweetest thing!
Oh, isn't she darling!
She's beautiful.
She's so big!
What an adorable baby!
His eyes are just like his father's.
Her nose looks just like her mother's.
She has her father's eyes.
He's got his mother's nose.

164 Asking about a new baby

How much does he weigh?
Was he early?
Was she late?
What's his name?
Who is she named after?
Has he been sleeping well?
Is she sleeping through the night?
Does he sleep through the night yet?
Can I hold her?
May I hold him?

165   Congratulating someone for doing a good job

Congratulations!
Good going!
Good job!
Good work!
Bravo!

166   Wishing someone well

Happy Birthday!
. . . and many (many) more!
Many happy returns!
Happy Anniversary!
Congratulations!
Good luck!
Best wishes!
All our best!
Bon voyage! (*French*)
   (*said when someone is leaving on a sea voyage*)
Have a good time!
Have a good trip!

167   Expressing sympathy at a funeral or wake

I'm sorry.
I'm so sorry.
I'm so sorry for your loss.
I'm very sorry.
You have my sympathy.
You have my deepest sympathy. (*formal*)
Please accept my sympathy. (*formal*)
My heart goes out to you.
I share your sorrow.
I share your pain.
How are you doing?

If you need anything, please let us know.

If there's anything we can do for you, please let us know.

Our thoughts are with you.

You're in our prayers.

We'll keep you in our prayers.

IMPOLITE ENCOUNTERS

Dealing with Unpleasantness

168   When someone is conceited or vain

You're so vain.

You're too big for your britches. (*informal*)

    britches = trousers

You're getting a little big for your britches. (*informal*)

Aren't you getting a little big for your britches? (*informal*)

You're so full of yourself. (*idiomatic*)

You think you're pretty smart, don't you? (*informal*)

You think you're so smart. (*informal*)

You think you're so big. (*informal*)

You think you're such a big shot. (*informal*)

    a big shot = an important person

You love the sound of your own voice. (*informal*)

You just like to hear yourself talk. (*informal*)

You talk just to hear yourself speak. (*informal*)

You think the world revolves around you.

The world doesn't revolve around you.

You think you're the center of the universe.

You're all wrapped up in yourself.

All you think about is yourself.

Did you ever stop to think about anyone else?

When someone is overbearing

Who died and made you king? (*informal*)
Who died and made you Pope? (*informal*)
Who died and made you God? (*informal*)
Smarty. (*informal*)
Smart-ass. (*mildly vulgar*)
Smarty pants. (*slang*)
Know-it-all. (*informal*)
Get off your high horse. (*informal*)
   = *Be less arrogant.*

Who do you think you are?
You think you're so smart? (*informal*)
You and who else? (*informal*)
You and what army? (*slang*)
What makes you so special? (*informal*)
Don't break your arm patting yourself on the back. (*idiomatic*)
You think you're so hot. (*informal*)
   hot = *important*

You think you're such hot stuff. (*informal*)
   hot stuff = *someone or something important*

When someone has been insolent or rude—shocked response

The nerve of you!
   nerve = *impudence; brashness*
What nerve you have!
You have a lot of nerve!
You've got a lot of nerve!
The nerve!
You have a lot of gall!
   gall = *nerve*
The gall!
The very idea!
How dare you!

Why, I never!
How could you say such a thing?
How could you do such a thing?
I beg your pardon!

171 When someone has been insolent or rude—firm response

Don't get smart with me!
Don't get sassy with me. (*folksy*)
  sassy = insolent

Don't sass me. (*folksy*)
Don't talk back to me.
Don't give me any of your lip. (*informal*)
  lip = insolent talk

Don't get uppity on me. (*folksy*)
  uppity = arrogant

Don't get uppity with me. (*folksy*)
Don't get cocky. (*informal*)
  cocky = insolent

Don't get fresh. (*informal*)
  fresh = insolent; impudent

Don't get your nose out of joint. (*informal*)
Don't overstep your bounds.
Watch yourself.
Watch it. (*informal*)
Watch out. (*informal*)

Don't get smart with me!

172 When someone has been insolent or rude—rude response

Oh, a smart aleck? (*informal*)
  a smart aleck = an insolent person

Oh, a wiseguy? (*slang*)
  a wiseguy = a smart aleck

Oh, a wiseacre? (*slang*)
  a wiseacre = a smart aleck

Oh, a smart-ass? (*mildly vulgar*)

   a smart-ass = a smart aleck

Oh, a smart mouth? (*slang*)

   a smart mouth = an impudent-talking smart aleck

Wiseguy. (*slang*)

Wiseacre. (*slang*)

Smart aleck. (*informal*)

Smart-ass. (*mildly vulgar*)

Wipe that grin off your face. (*informal*)

Wipe that smirk off your face. (*informal*)

173   Encouraging a timid person

Show a little resolve.

Show some courage.

Show some spine.

Don't be so spineless.

Don't be such a chicken-shit. (*taboo*)

   a chicken-shit = a coward

Don't be such a lily-liver. (*informal*)

   a lily-liver = a coward

174   Insulting a coward

Chicken! (*slang*)

   = *Coward!*

Wimp! (*slang*)

   = *Coward!*

Wuss! (*slang*)

   = *Coward!*

Fraidy-cat! (*juvenile*)

   a fraidy-cat = a coward

Scaredy-cat! (*juvenile*)

   a scaredy-cat = a coward

You're yellow. (*informal*)
  yellow = cowardly

You yellow-bellied sapsucker. (*informal*)
  = *You coward.*

You are a gutless wonder. (*slang*)
  gutless = cowardly

You're afraid of your own shadow. (*informal*)

Are you a man or a mouse? (*cliché*)

Cat got your tongue? (*cliché*)
  = *Are you afraid or unable to speak?*

Got cold feet?
  = *Are you too frightened to act?*

You really wimped out. (*slang*)
  wimped out = withdrew in a cowardly fashion

You really chickened out. (*slang*)
  chickened out = withdrew in a cowardly fashion

Lose your nerve?
  = *Did you lose your resolve?*

Are you a man or a mouse?

---

175   **When someone argues too much**

Don't contradict me.

You see everything in black and white.
  in black and white = in simple yes-no terms

If I said it was black, you'd say it was white.

That's as different as day and night.

It's (the difference between) apples and oranges.

You're just being contrary.

You're just disagreeing to disagree.

You're just disagreeing for the sake of disagreeing.

You're just playing the devil's advocate.

You're just arguing for the sake of arguing.

You just like to hear yourself talk.

176 When someone is being annoying

Would you stop that?
Could you please stop doing that?
You are really trying my patience.
That's really annoying.
That's really irritating.
That's driving me nuts! (*slang*)
That's making me crazy! (*informal*)
That's really bothersome.
That's really bothering me.
That's really bugging me. (*slang*)
    bugging = bothering
That's getting on my nerves. (*idiomatic*)
    getting on my nerves = annoying me
That's grating on my nerves.
    grating on my nerves = irritating me

You are really trying my patience!

177 Inviting an annoying person to leave

Scram! (*slang*)
    = *Get out!; Go away!*

Get lost. (*slang*)
Go blow. (*slang*)
Go fry an egg. (*slang*)
Go suck a lemon. (*slang*)
Go take a long walk off a short pier. (*informal*)
Go take a long walk on a short pier. (*informal*)
Make yourself scarce. (*slang*)
Go away!
Go climb a tree! (*slang*)
Go fly a kite! (*slang*)
Go jump in the lake! (*informal*)
(Go) jump off a cliff. (*informal*)
Go play in traffic! (*informal*)

Buzz off! (*slang*)
Bug off! (*slang*)
Scat! (*slang*)
Scram! (*slang*)
Shoo! (*informal*)
Take a hike! (*slang*)
Make like a tree and leave. (*informal*)
Get lost! (*slang*)
Get out of here! (*informal*)
Get out of my face! (*slang*)
Go blow. (*slang*)
Go play in traffic. (*informal*)

178   When someone is very annoying or hurtful

You really know what buttons to push!

Why don't you rub a little salt in the wound?
Why don't you twist the knife in my back?
You're going to be the death of me yet.
You'd try the patience of a saint.
You really get my goat.

> *to get my goat = to annoy me*

You're driving me up a wall.
You're driving me up the wall.
You really know what buttons to push.

> *what buttons to push = how to make me angry*

You're pushing my buttons.

179   Getting someone to stop doing something

Must you (do that)?
Must you continue to do that?
Stop bothering me.
Stop pestering me.
Quit pestering me.
Give it a rest. (*slang*)

> *it = your mouth*

Knock it off! (*slang*)

Cut it out! (*slang*)

Enough, already! (*informal*)

180   When someone is making you angry—rude

I'm really upset with you right now.

Get a life! (*slang*)

Get a clue! (*slang*)

You're pissing me off. (*mildly vulgar*)

I'm really getting P.O.'d. (*mildly vulgar*)

 P.O.'d = pissed off = angry

181   Asking to be left alone

Let me be.

Let me alone.

Leave me be.

Please go away.

Please leave me alone.

I'm asking you to leave me alone.

I just want to be left alone.

182   Describing a bothersome person

You're a pain in the neck. (*slang*)

You're a pain in the ass. (*mildly vulgar*)

You're a pain in the butt. (*mildly vulgar*)

You're a royal pain. (*slang*)

You're a pain. (*slang*)

He grates on me.

He grates on my nerves.

 grates on my nerves = annoys me

He gets on my nerves.

He pushes my buttons.

He rubs me the wrong way.

You're a royal pain!

He gets my dander up. (*informal*)

dander = temper

He raises my hackles.

hackles = long hairs at the back of the neck = temper

183   When someone has done something wrong—polite

How could you do such a silly thing?
How could you do such a thing?
What could you have been thinking?
What on earth were you thinking?
What possessed you to do that?
What got into you?
I hope you're sorry.
When will you ever learn?
Now what did you go and do that for? (*folksy*)

184   When someone has done something wrong—amazed

Are you out of your mind?
Are you crazy?
Have you taken leave of your senses?
If I've told you once, I've told you a hundred times. (*informal*)
If I've told you once, I've told you a thousand times. (*informal*)
I can't believe you embarrassed me like that!
If that's what you think, you've got another think coming. (*informal*)
You've got another think coming. (*informal*)

185   When someone has done something wrong—sarcastic

Are you happy (now)?
Are you satisfied?
I hope you're happy.
I hope you're satisfied.
Aren't you proud of yourself?
I hope you're proud of yourself.

186   When someone makes an unwelcome intervention

Who asked you? (*informal*)

Who asked your opinion?

When I want your opinion, I'll ask for it.

Who invited you?

You're not invited.

You're not welcome here.

We don't want your kind around here.

187   Telling someone to stay away or keep out

Keep out.

No trespassing.

Members only.

Employees only.

No admittance.

No admittance without proper identification. (*formal*)

These premises are for the use of members and guests only. (*formal*)

188   Asking someone's intentions

You got a problem? (*informal*)

What do you mean by that?

Were you talking to me?

Are you trying to start something?

(Just exactly) what are you getting at?

(Just exactly) what are you trying to say?

189   Starting a fight

Do you want to step outside (and settle this)?

Would you like to step outside?

Want to make something of it?

    something = an issue to fight about

Care to make something of it?

190   Asking someone to leave your property alone

Hands off!
Excuse me, that's mine.
Did I say you could touch that?
Look with your eyes not your hands.
If you break it, you pay for it.
If you break it, you've bought it.

191   Asking someone to stay out of your affairs

Mind your own business. (*informal*)
Mind your own beeswax. (*slang*)
    beeswax = business
M.Y.O.B. (*slang*)
    = *Mind your own business.*
Butt out! (*slang*)
    = *Mind your own business!*
That's none of your affair.
Get your nose out of my business. (*informal*)
Keep your nose out of my business. (*informal*)

Mind your own business!

192   When someone is harassing you—angry and direct

Get off my back! (*slang*)
Lay off, will you! (*slang*)
Get off my tail! (*slang*)
Get off my ass! (*mildly vulgar*)
Get off it! (*slang*)
Come off it! (*slang*)

193   When someone is harassing you—rude

Nuts to you. (*mildly vulgar*)
Screw you. (*mildly vulgar*)
Up yours. (*vulgar*)

194 When someone is presumptuous

Why would you ask such a thing?
How could you say such a thing?
What right do you have to say that?
Who gave you the right?
Where do you come off saying that?
Well, I never!

195 When someone has underestimated your intelligence

How dumb do you think I am? (*informal*)
Do you think I was born yesterday? (*informal*)
Who do you think you're kidding? (*informal*)
Who do you think you're talking to? (*informal*)

196 When someone interrupts with an opinion

Was I talking to you?
Who asked you?
I wasn't speaking to you.
When I want your opinion, I'll ask it.
When I want your opinion, I'll beat it out of you. (*jocular*)
Thank you for sharing. (*sarcastic*)
I'll thank you to keep your opinions to yourself.
I'll thank you to mind your own business!
Keep your nose out of my business. (*informal*)
Keep your opinions to yourself.
Mind your own business.
Mind your own beeswax. (*slang*)
    beeswax = business
M.Y.O.B. (*slang*)
    = Mind your own business.

197   Apologizing—sarcastic

Well, excuse me. (*informal*)
Excuse me for breathing. (*informal*)
Excuse me for living. (*informal*)
Pardon me for living. (*informal*)

198   When someone overreacts

Relax.
Chill. (*informal*)
Don't get bent out of shape. (*slang*)
Don't make a federal case out of it. (*informal*)
Like it's such a big deal. (*informal*)
It's no big deal. (*informal*)
You're making a mountain out of a molehill.
Don't bite my head off. (*informal*)
Don't jump down my throat. (*informal*)
Same to you. (*informal*)
So's your uncle. (*informal*)
Sue me. (*informal*)
So, sue me. (*informal*)

199   When punishment is in store for someone

You'll get yours.
You'll get your due.
You'll get what's coming to you.
What goes around comes around. (*cliché*)
You'll get your just deserts.

200   Explaining harsh justice

What goes around comes around. (*cliché*)
It cuts both ways. (*cliché*)

Quid pro quo. (*Latin*)
  = *This for that.*

An eye for an eye; a tooth for a tooth.

The chickens have come home to roost.

Two can play (at) that game. (*informal*)

Serves you right.

201 Threatening retaliation

I'll give you a dose of your own medicine. (*cliché*)

I'll fix your wagon. (*cliché*)

I dare you.

Go ahead, make my day. (*cliché*)

202 Requesting silence

Quiet!

Be quiet!

Keep quiet!

Keep still!

Be still!

Hush!

Silence! (*formal*)

Shut up! (*informal*)

Shut your mouth! (*informal*)

Shut your trap! (*informal*)

Hold your tongue!

Hush your mouth! (*informal*)

Shush! (*informal*)

Shh! (*informal*)

Not another word!

Button your lip! (*informal*)

Button in! (*informal*)

Clam up! (*slang*)

Dry up! (*slang*)

Keep quiet!

203   Requesting someone to stop needless talk

Can it! (*slang*)

Stow it! (*slang*)

Put a cork in it! (*slang*)
> it = your mouth

Put a sock in it! (*slang*)

Cut the gab! (*slang*)
> gab = needless chatter

Cut the crap! (*mildly vulgar*)
> crap = dung = needless chatter

> You're not reaching your potential.

204   When someone is not doing enough

You're not doing your share.

You're not doing your fair share.

You're not carrying your weight.

You're not pulling your weight.

You're not pulling your own weight.

You're not living up to your end of the bargain.

You're not holding up your end of the bargain.

You're not reaching your potential.

You're slacking off.

Get on the stick. (*slang*)

205   When someone starts trouble

Stop stirring things up.

You like to make trouble, don't you?

Don't you have anything better to do?

You've got too much time on your hands.

Can't you leave well enough alone?

Get a job! (*slang*)

Get a hobby! (*informal*)

Get a life! (*slang*)

Aw, poor baby.
You poor thing.
My heart bleeds for you.
I'm all choked up.

207   **Expressing mock sympathy—sarcastic**

Here's a quarter. Call someone who cares.
Obviously you've mistaken me for someone who cares.
What makes you think I care?
Do you think I care?
Like I care. (*informal*)
As if I care. (*informal*)
As if. (*informal*)
Frankly, my dear, I don't give a damn. (*mildly vulgar*)
Good for you.
I'm happy for you.
Thanks for sharing.
I'm so glad you told us that.
Thank you for sharing.
Isn't that special?

208   **When you are helpless to help—rude**

What do you want me to do about it?
What do you expect me to do about it?
What am I supposed to do about it?
Like I can do anything about it.

VISITS

Guests and Hosts

209 **Asking to visit someone**

Are you free later today?

Could I come over later today?

Can I come over?

Do you mind if I stop by later today?

Would you mind if I stopped by later?

Would it be a problem if I dropped by for a few minutes?

Would it be all right if I dropped by for a few minutes?

Are you busy or can I come over?

When would be a good time for me to come over?

When's a good time for you?

I'll be there by seven.

I'll be there after dinner.

210 **When you are invited to an informal meal in a home**

Do I need to bring anything?

Would you like me to bring anything?

Can I bring something?

Can I bring anything?

Should I bring anything?

What should I bring?

Would you like me to bring wine?

Shall I bring wine?

I'll bring the wine.

Let me bring dessert.

Would you like me to bring wine?

211   Asking about an invitation you have received

What time should I be there?
What do you have planned?
How should I dress?
What should I wear?
Is it casual or formal?
I'm planning to drive. How's the parking?
Can I bring my kids?
May I bring a friend?
Can I bring something?
  something = food

212   Apologizing for being late

I'm sorry I'm late.
Sorry I'm late.
I'm sorry to have kept you waiting.
Sorry to have kept you waiting.

213   Explaining why one is late

I misjudged the time.
I didn't realize it was so late.
I lost track of time.
I overslept.
My alarm didn't go off.
I got a late start.
I got sidetracked.
  sidetracked = detoured; distracted
My last appointment ran over.
I had to run an errand.
I had to drop someone off.
I had to get money.
I couldn't get a taxi.
I couldn't get a cab.

The train was late.

The bus was late.

I missed the bus.

I missed my ride.

My ride didn't show (up).

I had to get gas.

I had to stop for gas.

I had to stop and get gas.

I ran out of gas.

Traffic was slow.

Traffic was hell. (*mildly vulgar*)

I was stuck in traffic.

I got lost.

I don't have GPS.

I missed my exit.

There was construction.

There was an accident.

It took me longer to get here than I thought it would.

It took longer than I expected to get here.

I didn't realize this was so far away.

It was farther than I thought.

I was looking for parking.

I couldn't find a parking spot.

I couldn't find a parking place.

I couldn't find a place to park.

214   When you finally arrive after being late

I hope you started without me.

I'm glad you started without me.

Were you waiting long?

You should have started without me.

Next time start without me.

215 Greetings for visitors

Look who's here!

Well, look who's here!

Am I surprised to see you!

Am I ever surprised to see you!

Look at what the cat dragged in! (*folksy*)

Fancy meeting you here.

216 Inviting a visitor to come in

Come on in.

Come right on in.

Come right in.

Do come in. (*formal*)

Please come in.

Come in and relax for a few minutes.

Come in and take a load off your feet. (*folksy*)

Come in and take a load off. (*folksy*)

Come in and sit down.

Come in and set a spell. (*folksy*)

Come in and stay a while.

Come in and make yourself at home.

217 After greeting a visitor

To what do I owe the pleasure of this unexpected visit? (*formal*)

To what do I owe this visit?

What are you doing here?

What brings you here?

What brings you to this neck of the woods? (*folksy*)

    neck of the woods = location

Why this delightful surprise?

What a delightful surprise!

What a nice surprise!

It's nice to see you again.

It's a pleasure to see you again. (*formal*)

It's so good to see you again.

It's so good to see you after all this time.

Good seeing you again.

I'm delighted to have you visit.

I'm delighted to have you.

Delighted to have you here.

I'm so happy you looked me up.

I'm so glad you looked me up.

I'm so glad you took the trouble to look me up.

I'm so glad you could come.

I'm so glad you could come by.

I'm so glad you could make it.

I'm so glad you could drop by.

I'm so glad you could stop by.

I'm so glad you could visit.

Glad you could come.

Glad you could drop by.

Glad you could stop by.

We've wanted to have you over before this.

We've wanted to invite you over before this.

We've been meaning to have you over.

We've been meaning to invite you over.

We've been looking forward to seeing you for a long time.

We've been wanting to see you for a long time.

218   Making a visitor feel welcome and comfortable

Make yourself comfortable.

Make yourself comfy.

Make yourself right at home.

Make yourself at home.

Would you like to take off your coat?

Here, let me take your coat.

Can I take your coat and hat?

Can I help you off with your things?

Let me help you off with your things.

Take your coat off and stay awhile.

Why don't you take off your coat and make yourself comfortable?

Put your things anywhere and sit down for a minute.

Just drop your coat here. (*informal*)

219   Inviting a visitor to stay for dinner

Can you stay for dinner?

> *Can you = Would you, Are you able to, Will you*

Can you have dinner with us?

Can you stay and have dinner with us?

Would you care to stay for dinner?

Can you stay and have dinner with us?

220   Encouraging a guest to feel at home

Please make yourself at home.

Our house is your house.

My house is your house.

Mi casa es su casa. (*Spanish*)

If there's anything you need, don't hesitate to ask.

If there's anything you want, don't hesitate to ask.

If there's anything I can do for you, just ask.

You're to do exactly as you please.

Please do exactly as you please.

Would you like to freshen up a bit?

Would you like something to drink?

Can I get you something to drink?

221   Offering a guest a seat

Please sit down.

Have a seat.

Try this chair. It's more comfortable.

Would you like to sit over here?

Would you prefer a more comfortable chair?

222   Steering a guest to a particular room

Please come into the living room.

Come on in the living room.

Right this way. Everyone seems to be in the kitchen.

The other guests are in the library.

Would you like to join us in the living room?

Everyone is in the living room. Would you care to join us?

223   Encouraging a guest to be independent

Please go around and introduce yourself to everyone.

Could you just introduce yourself to the other guests?

Just go in and meet everyone.

I hope you don't mind introducing yourself around.

Don't stand on ceremony. Make yourself known.

Get yourself a drink and something to eat.

Please feel free to mingle with the other guests.

I hope you don't mind getting yourself a drink.

The bar's over there. Please help yourself.

224   Mingling with other guests

Mind if I join you?

Care if I join you?

May I join you?

Hello, my name is Lee.

Hello, I'm Jane.

So how do you know Juan and Maria?

I work with Juan.

I'm friends with Maria.

I'm a friend of Maria's.

Have you tried the dip?

Great party, huh? (*informal*)

What a great spread!

    spread = display of party food

225　What a guest says to a host or hostess

Where can I put my coat?
Do you mind if I smoke?
Mind if I smoke?
Where is the bathroom (, please)?
You have a beautiful home.
The table looks beautiful.
I love what you have done with the living room.
You have a wonderful place.
You have wonderful taste.

226　Starting a conversation using the topic of weather

Nice weather we're having.
Lousy weather, isn't it?
Horrible weather we're having.
Lovely weather for ducks. (*sarcastic*)
It's raining again.
Hot enough for you? (*ironic*)
Cold enough for you? (*ironic*)
It's not the heat; it's the humidity. (*cliché*)

227　Asking a question to start a conversation

What's new?
What's up?
What time is it?
Do you have the time?
This food is good, isn't it?

228　Starting a conversation with someone you know well

How have you been?
How's work?
How's your family?

How's the family?
Looks like you just got a haircut.
I like your hair.
I like your outfit.
That dress is lovely.
That dress looks nice on you.
Where did you buy that sweater? I've been wanting to get one.

229   Starting a conversation in a waiting room

Can I take a look at your paper?
What are you listening to?
What book are you reading?
Read any good books lately?
Did you see that show last night?
Seen any good movies recently?
Do you have a breath mint?
I'm going to get a coffee. Would you like one?

230   Talking about the weather

Nice weather we're having.
The sun is shining.
It's bright and sunny.
It's eighty degrees.
Lousy weather, huh?
Horrible weather we're having.
Lovely weather for ducks. (*sarcastic*)
It's not the heat; it's the humidity. (*cliché*)
It's raining again.
It's raining cats and dogs. (*cliché*)
What a storm!
What a downpour!
What a snowstorm!
What a blizzard!
Hot enough for you? (*ironic*)

Cold enough for you? (*ironic*)

It's raining.

It's snowing.

It's cold.

It's hot.

It's humid.

It's foggy.

It's smoggy.

It's muggy.

It's windy.

231   What to say when in a crowded place

It's too crowded in here.

I feel like a sardine.

We're packed in like sardines.

We're crammed in like sardines.

We're crammed solid.

This party is wall-to-wall people.

It's absolutely jam-packed.

I'm getting claustrophobic.

I need some elbowroom.

There's no room to breathe.

There's not enough room to swing a cat. (*folksy*)

Would you like to go somewhere quieter?

Would you like to go somewhere less crowded?

232   Preparing to leave home

Do we have everything?

Have we forgotten anything?

Did we forget anything?

Do you have your keys?

Did you leave a light on?

I can't find my keys.

Wait, I forgot my wallet.

Did you bring the map?
Do you have the directions?
Are the kids ready?
Is the answering machine on?
Did you go to the bathroom?
Did you unplug the iron?
Did you turn off the TV?
Did you turn down the heating?
Did you turn off the stove?

233   **Stating when you will return home**

I'll be gone just a few minutes.
See you in an hour.
I won't be late.
I'll be back by ten.
I'll be home late.
Don't wait up for me.

234   **Preparing to leave a host or hostess**

Well, it's getting late.
Is it that late already?
Is it that time already?
Looks like it's that time.
The time has come.
I hate to eat and run.
I don't want to wear out my welcome.
I need my beauty sleep. (*jocular*)
We have to get up early tomorrow.
We have a big day tomorrow.
    big = busy
I need to run.
I'm afraid I must run.
I'm afraid I must be going.
I've got to be running.

I'm afraid I have to be going.

I've got to be going.

I'd better be off.

I'd best be off.

I'd best leave now.

I better get moving.

I better hit the road.

I must be off.

I must say good night.

I've got to hit the road. (*idiomatic*)

I better get on my horse. (*idiomatic*)

I'm off. (*informal*)

I'm out of here. (*slang*)

I'm history. (*slang*)

Better be going.

Better be off.

Better get moving.

Better hit the road. (*idiomatic*)

Time to call it a day.

Time to call it a night.

Time to go.

Time to run.

Time to hit the road.

Time to move along.

Time to push along.

Time to push off.

Time to shove off.

Time to split. (*slang*)

Time flies when you're having fun. (*cliché*)

Gotta go.

Got to hit the road.

Got to run.

Got to shove off.

Got to split. (*slang*)

Got to take off.

Got to be shoving off.

Got to fly.

Got to get moving.

Got to go home and get my beauty sleep. (*jocular*)

Have to be moving along.

Have to go now.

Have to move along.

Have to run along.

Have to shove off.

235　When departing

Thanks for having me over.

Thank you for a lovely evening. (*formal*)

Thank you for a lovely time. (*formal*)

Thank you for having us.

Thank you for inviting us.

236　Questions asked of departing guests

Do you want a cup of coffee before you go?

Are you sober enough to drive?

Can I call you a taxi?

Can you find your way home?

Will you get home all right?

Will you get home okay? (*informal*)

Do you have everything?

　　everything = everything that you arrived with

237　Saying good-bye to departing guests

It's been a delightful visit. (*formal*)

It's been delightful.

It's been our pleasure.

So good to see you.

Do you have everything?

Thank you for coming.

So good to see you.

We have to do this again sometime.

Thanks for coming.
Thanks for dropping in.
Thanks for dropping by.
Thanks for stopping over.
I'm so glad you stopped by.
Glad you could come.
Glad you could drop by.
Glad you could stop by.
Come back soon.
Come back anytime.
Come back when you can stay longer.
Do come back soon.
Let's do this again soon.
We have to do this again sometime.
See you soon.

MISCELLANEOUS EXPRESSIONS

Comments and Phrases

238   **General exclamations**

Wow!
Gosh!
Golly!
Gee!
Gee whiz!
Holy cow!
Holy crap! (*vulgar*)
Holy shit! (*vulgar*)
Holy smoke!
Holy Toledo!

Son of a gun!

Son of a bitch! (*mildly vulgar*)

Son of a sea biscuit!

Well, I'll be!

I'll be darned!

I'll be damned! (*mildly vulgar*)

Well, I'll be a monkey's uncle!

What do you know?

Imagine that!

Can you beat that!

Fancy that!

Isn't that something!

Well if that ain't the cats' meow.

By gum! (*folksy*)

By golly! (*folksy*)

By Jove!

By George!

Great Scott!

Oh, my!

My word!

Oh, my goodness!

My goodness!

Goodness!

Heavens!

Good heavens!

For heaven's sake!

For Pete's sake!

For pity's sake!

Good gracious!

Good grief!

Goodness gracious!

My God! (*oath*)

Oh my God! (*oath*)

God forbid! (*mild oath*)

Great!

Excellent!

Hot dog!

Hot diggety! (*folksy*)

Good Lord!

Hot damn! (*mildly vulgar*)

Lordy! (*mild oath*)

Lordy be! (*mild oath*)

Lord have mercy! (*mild oath*)

Saints preserve us! (*mild oath*)

Glory be!

Hush my mouth! (*folksy*)

Shut my mouth! (*folksy*)

As I live and breathe!

My stars!

Zounds!

Gadzooks!

You don't say!

Will wonders never cease!

239   Religious expressions

Amen!

    = *I agree!*

Hallelujah!

    = *Hooray!*

Alleluia!

    = *Hooray!*

Hosanna!

    = *Hooray!*

Glory (be) to God!

Praise be to God!

Thanks be to God.

240   Expressions meaning "almost"

Nice try. (*sarcastic*)

Not quite.

So near and yet so far.

So close and yet so far.

Close, but no cigar. (*cliché*)

You were within a hair's breadth.

Close enough for government work. (*informal*)

Almost only counts in horseshoes and hand grenades. (*cliché*)

It's all or nothing.

A miss is as good as a mile. (*cliché*)

241   Leaving things as they are

Let it be.

Leave it be.

Let it go.

Let things be.

Live and let live.

If it ain't broke, don't fix it. (*cliché*)

Let sleeping dogs lie. (*cliché*)

Don't make waves. (*idiomatic*)

Don't rock the boat. (*idiomatic*)

Don't make trouble.

Don't go looking for trouble.

242   Expressing differences between people—clichés

Different strokes for different folks.

We'll agree to disagree.

One man's meat is another man's poison.

One man's trash is another man's treasure.

Tastes differ.

There's no accounting for taste.

Variety is the spice of life.

It takes all kinds.

It takes all kinds to make a world.

Vive la difference! (*French*)

    = *Hooray for the difference!*

243   Warnings

Be prepared!

Be careful!

Watch out!

Watch it!

Look out!

Look sharp!

Watch your step!

Heads up!

Behind you!

To your right!

On your left!

Coming through!

Gangway!

Make way!

Fore!

    (*said in golfing when the ball is struck*)

Duck!

Hit the pavement!

Hit the deck!

Beware!

Caution!

Proceed with caution.

Man overboard!

    (*said when someone falls from a boat into the water*)

Fire!

Take care.

Safety first.

Look before you leap.

Let's take this one step at a time. (*cliché*)

Leave nothing to chance. (*cliché*)

Slow down.

Take your time.

Play it cool.

Play it safe.

Don't blow your cover.

Stop, look, and listen.

Look both ways before you cross the street.

Let the buyer beware.

Caveat emptor. (*Latin*)

 = *Let the buyer beware.*

We're not out of the woods yet. (*idiomatic*)

We're skating on thin ice.

244 Giving and receiving—clichés

What goes around, comes around.

You scratch my back, I'll scratch yours.

One hand washes the other.

Do unto others as you would have them do unto you.

Do as you would be done by.

As a man sows, so shall he reap.

Tit for tat.

 = *This in return for that.*

Quid pro quo. (*Latin*)

 = *Tit for tat.*

245 Cause and effect—clichés

April showers bring May flowers.

You made your bed; now lie in it.

As the twig is bent, so is the tree inclined.

As the twig is bent, so grows the tree.

One good turn deserves another.

One thing leads to another.

It's not over 'til it's over.
Boys will be boys.
East is east, west is west.
That's that.
Life is life.
That's life.
Enough is enough.

247   **Expressions for a forgotten word or name**

Whatsit.
Whaddya call it.
Whatchamacallit.
Whatchamajig.
Thingamajig.
Thingamajigger.
What's 'er name.
What's 'is name.
What's 'is face.
What's 'er face.
You know who.
You know what I mean.
That certain something.
Je ne sais quoi. (*French*)
    = *I don't know.*

248   **Regarding order and procedure**

There is a time and a place for everything. (*cliché*)
A place for everything and everything in its place. (*cliché*)
Everything has its season. (*cliché*)
All in due time. (*cliché*)
First things first. (*cliché*)
First come, first served. (*cliché*)

The first shall be last and the last shall be first. (*Biblical*)

Rules are made to be broken. (*cliché*)

Rules are meant to be followed, not broken.

When in Rome, do as the Romans do. (*cliché*)

Don't put the cart before the horse. (*cliché*)

Don't count your chickens before they are hatched. (*cliché*)

Let's cross that bridge when we come to it. (*cliché*)

Do what you are told.

Do as you are told.

I just do what I am told.

I just do as I am told.

I just work here.

I'm just the help.

Follow the rules.

That's how we do it here.

Go by the book.

You must go through proper channels.

249   Describing a messy place

This place is a mess.

This place is a pigsty.

This place is a disgrace.

What a mess.

What a pit. (*slang*)

What a dump. (*slang*)

What a junk heap. (*slang*)

This place looks like a tornado hit it.

This place looks like a national disaster (area).

This place looks like a disaster area.

This place looks like it went through the war.

This place looks like it's been through a war.

This place looks like it's been through World War III.

How can you find anything in here?

How do you expect to find anything in this mess?

Were you raised in a barn?

How about cleaning up a little around here?

If you would put things where they belong, they wouldn't get lost.

250   Concerning unity—clichés

United we stand; divided we fall.

A house divided against itself cannot stand.

All for one and one for all.

Birds of a feather flock together.

Many hands make light work.

251   Concerning nostalgia

When I was a kid . . .

When I was your age . . .

In my day . . .

In my time . . .

In that day and age . . .

Those were the days.

Those were the good old days.

They don't make them like they used to.

252   Concerning strength—clichés

You don't know your own strength.

You're as strong as an ox.

A chain is only as strong as its weakest link.

253   Concerning rigidity of character—idioms and clichés

He's set in his ways.

A leopard cannot change his spots.

You can't teach an old dog new tricks.

Old habits die hard.

You're as stubborn as a bull.

Why are you so bullheaded?

254 Feeling warm or hot

It's hot in here.
It's like an oven in here.
I'm sweltering.
I'm going to melt.
Open a window.
Turn on the air conditioner.
Hot enough for you? (*ironic*)
Is it hot enough for you? (*ironic*)
It's not the heat, it's the humidity. (*cliché*)
It's as hot as hell. (*mildly vulgar*)

255 Feeling cool or cold

It's cold in here.
I'm freezing.
I'm shivering.
My teeth are chattering.
My lips are blue.
I'm going numb.
I'm chilled to the bone.
Shut the window.
Turn on the heat.
Turn up the heat.
Turn the heat up.
Cold enough for you? (*ironic*)
Is it cold enough for you? (*ironic*)

256 Describing additional unspecified people or things

Et cetera. (*Latin*)
   = *And so forth.*
And so on.
And so forth.
And everything.

And everything else.
And everything like that.
And all like that.
And stuff. (*slang*)
And stuff like that (there). (*slang*)
And what have you.
And like that.
And then some.

257 Concerning cleanliness

It's as clean as a whistle.
It's so clean you could eat off the floor.
It's spic and span.
Clean your room.
Pick up your clothes.
I want you to pick up your room.
I want this place spotless.
Pick up after yourself.
Were you raised in a barn?
You live like a pig!
A place for everything, and everything in its place. (*cliché*)
Cleanliness is next to godliness. (*cliché*)

258 Concerning surprise

Unbelievable!
I had no idea!
Who would have thought?
It was the last thing I expected.
I never would have guessed.
I was caught unaware.
I was caught unawares. (*informal*)
It was the shock of my life.
It dropped like a bomb.
It dropped from the clouds.

It appeared from the clouds.

It burst onto the scene.

It came out of left field.

It came from nowhere.

It appeared out of nowhere.

It came from out of the blue.

It was a bolt from the blue.

It threw me for a loop.

That knocked me for a loop.

You could have knocked me over with a feather. (*cliché*)

259   Concerning expectation

It came as no surprise.

I knew it was coming.

It's just as I expected.

My fingers are crossed.

I'm crossing my fingers.

I'm waiting with bated breath. (*cliché*)

I'll wait for you.

I'll stay up for you.

I'll wait up.

I'll sit up and wait.

I'm crossing my fingers!

260   Concerning a premonition

I have a hunch.

I have a feeling.

I have a gut feeling.

I just have this feeling.

I get the feeling something's going to happen.

I feel it in my bones.

I can feel it.

I can sense it.

My sixth sense tells me that . . .

My gut tells me that . . .

It's women's intuition.

A storm is brewing.

The handwriting's on the wall. (*cliché*)

It's an omen.

It's a harbinger of things to come.

It's a sign of things to come.

It's a portent of things to come.

It's a good sign.

It's a bad sign.

It's a good omen.

It's a bad omen.

261   Concerning being busy—clichés

You're as busy as a beaver.

You're as busy as a bee.

Many hands make light work.

A little work never hurt anyone.

It's all in a day's work.

A woman's work is never done.

All work and no play makes Jack a dull boy.

God helps those who help themselves.

262   Making an extra effort

I've gone out of my way to please you.

I've bent over backwards for you.

I've gone the extra mile.

I've gone beyond the call of duty.

I've gone above and beyond the call of duty.

You've gotten the royal treatment.

I've treated you like a king.

I've treated you like a queen.

We've rolled out the red carpet. (*idiomatic*)

= *We've prepared for the event as if we were preparing for royalty.*

You're getting the red-carpet treatment. (*idiomatic*)
    red-carpet = royal

We aim to please.

We aim to treat you right. (*folksy*)

263   Demanding to be given an object

Give it to me.

Give it here. (*informal*)

Give it up. (*informal*)

Gimme it. (*informal*)

Gimme. (*informal*)

Give. (*informal*)

Cough it up. (*informal*)
    it = money

Hand it over. (*informal*)

Fork it over. (*slang*)

Let me have it.

Where is it?

Leave it go. (*informal*)

Let it go.

Let go of that.

264   When someone is preparing for an important event—clichés

This is your big night.

This could be your lucky day.

This is it.

This is the moment you've been waiting for.

This is the big moment.

Knock 'em dead. (*informal*)

Break a leg. (*informal*)
    (*a way of wishing good luck to an actor before a performance*)

Make us proud of you.

Make us proud.

I'm sure you will make us proud of you.

265   When someone is dressed up

You're dressed to the nines. (*slang*)

You're dressed to kill. (*slang*)

You're all dressed up.

You're all gussied up. (*informal*)
    gussied up = dressed up (male or female)

You're all dolled up. (*informal*)
    dolled up = dressed up like a doll (male or female)

You look great in a monkey suit. (*informal*)
    monkey suit = tuxedo; evening jacket (usually male)

You look like a million bucks.

You look like a million dollars.

You look like a million.

You look a million.

266   When you feel you are not wanted

Do you want me to go (away)?

Do you want me to leave?

Would you like me to leave?

If you want me to leave, just ask.

If you want me to leave, why don't you just say so?

I know when I'm not wanted.

I don't like being here any better than you do.

Am I cramping your style? (*informal*)

267   Regarding something less than what was desired

I was hoping for more.

I was counting on more.

I was gunning for more.

It's not what I had in mind.

It's not what I pictured.

It's not what I hoped for.

It's not what I had hoped for.

It's not what I expected.

It's not what I anticipated.

I expected something more.

It's a far cry from what I expected.

It leaves a lot to be desired.

They got the best of me.

I've been cheated.

I didn't get what I bargained for.

I was taken advantage of.

I got left holding the bag.

> I got = I've been, I was

I got gypped. (*informal*)

> gypped = cheated

I got rooked. (*informal*)

> rooked = cheated

I got the short end of the stick.

> the short end of the stick = the losing part of a bargain

I got robbed. (*informal*)

I got taken. (*informal*)

I got taken to the cleaners. (*informal*)

I got a bum deal. (*informal*)

> a bum deal = a bad deal; an unfair deal

I got a raw deal. (*informal*)

> a raw deal = a bad deal; an unfair deal

I got screwed. (*mildly vulgar*)

268 Describing a reprimand

I got chewed out. (*informal*)

> I got = I've been, I was

I got my ass chewed out. (*mildly vulgar*)

I got raked over the coals. (*idiomatic*)

I got hauled over the coals. (*idiomatic*)

I got an earful.

I was put through the wringer.

I was taken to task.

They let me off the hook this time. (*idiomatic*)

    off the hook = free from an obligation or guilt

They let me off easy.

They let me off with just a warning.

They let it slide.

They let it go.

I just got a slap on the wrist.

    a slap on the wrist = a mild punishment

269   When something is broken

It broke.

It's broken.

It doesn't work.

It's on the fritz. (*idiomatic*)

    on the fritz = out of order

It's on the blink. (*informal*)

    on the blink = out of order

This thing is really screwed up! (*informal*)

    screwed up = messed up; made to be out of order

270   When something is out of order

It's out of order.

It's out of service.

It's out of kilter. (*informal*)

It's out of whack. (*informal*)

It's dead. (*informal*)

It's kaput. (*slang*)

    kaput (German) = dead

It up and died (on me). (*folksy*)

It died on me.

It's in the shop.

> *in the shop = in the repair shop*

It's out of commission.

271   On being pushed to the limit of your patience

That's the straw that broke the camel's back. (*cliché*)

> = *That's the minor thing that will finally trigger some activity.*

That's the last straw! (*cliché*)

> *the last straw = the straw that broke the camel's back*

That does it!

That's it.

I've had it.

That tears it. (*idiomatic*)

This is too much.

This is more than I can bear.

This is more than I can take.

This is more than I can stand.

That's just what I needed.

I needed that like a hole in
> the head. (*sarcastic*)

That's a fine how-do-you-do.

Here's a fine how-do-you-do.

Well, that takes the cake!
> (*idiomatic*)

That's just swell! (*sarcastic*)

That's just great! (*sarcastic*)

Now what?

> = *What else could possibly happen at this point?*

272   Beginning a new project or activity

Where do we begin?

How should we go about doing this?

What's the first step?

What's first on the agenda?

Let's organize a task force.

Who will be in charge?

We're on our way.

We're off and running.

We're off to a good start.

We've hit the ground running.

We're headed in the right direction.

We're off on the right foot.

We've laid a good foundation.

We've only just begun.

We're just getting our feet wet. (*idiomatic*)

    getting our feet wet = just getting started

We've made a good dent in it. (*idiomatic*)

It's a start.

You've got to begin somewhere.

I'd like to lay down a few ground rules.

273   Concerning the deceptively difficult

It's not as easy as it seems.

It's not as easy as it looks.

It's harder than it looks.

It's harder than you think.

Easier said than done.

There's more to it than meets the eye.

It's surprisingly difficult.

It's like looking for a needle in a haystack.

It's a real challenge.

274 Concerning the impossible

That won't work.
That'll never hold water.
  = *That will never be operable.*
Never happen. (*informal*)
There's no way. (*informal*)
No can do. (*informal*)

275 Concerning futility

You're wasting your time.
You're wasting your energy.
You're wasting your effort.
It doesn't stand a chance.
It doesn't stand a chance in hell. (*mildly vulgar*)
There's not a chance in hell. (*mildly vulgar*)
It doesn't stand a snowball's chance in hell. (*mildly vulgar*)
When hell freezes over. (*mildly vulgar*)
  = *Never.*

You're spinning your wheels. (*informal*)
You're (just) running around in circles.
You're beating a dead horse. (*informal*)
  *beating a dead horse = trying to activate or motivate something that
    is finished*
It isn't worth beating your brains out (for). (*informal*)
It's like looking for a needle in a haystack. (*cliché*)
It's fit for the junkyard.
It's headed for the junk heap. (*informal*)

276 When something is unimportant

It doesn't matter.
It makes no difference.
It makes no nevermind. (*folksy*)
  = *It doesn't matter to me.*

It don't make (me) no nevermind. (*folksy*)

It's six of one, half a dozen of the other.

> = *It doesn't matter which one or which way.*

It's not important.

It's not worthwhile.

It's not worth your while.

It's not worth a hill of beans. (*idiomatic*)

It's not worth mentioning.

It's not worth the trouble.

It's not worth it.

277 Ending a project

Get rid of it.

Finish it off.

Nip it in the bud.

Do it in. (*informal*)

86 it. (*slang*)

> 86 = *nix* = *to negate; to destroy*

Kill it. (*informal*)

Kill it off. (*informal*)

Wipe it out. (*informal*)

Wipe it off the map. (*informal*)

Sound the death knell. (*informal*)

> *the death knell = the sound of bells that signals an impending or recent death*

Put it out of its misery. (*informal*)

Pull the plug on it. (*slang*)

Pull the rug out from under it. (*informal*)

Put the skids on it. (*informal*)

Nuke it. (*slang*)

> = *Destroy it with a nuclear bomb.*

Throw it away.

Throw it out.

Pitch it. (*informal*)

Toss it. (*informal*)

Junk it. (*informal*)

Trash it. (*informal*)

Dump it. (*informal*)

Put it in the circular file. (*informal*)

　　the circular file = a (round) wastebasket

File it in the circular bin. (*informal*)

　　the circular bin = the circular file; a (round) wastebasket

File it. (*informal*)

278　Starting over again on a project

Back to the drawing board.

It's back to the drawing board.

Well, it's back to square one.

Well, it's back to basics.

Time to start over from scratch.

PERSONAL MATTERS

Feelings

279　Asking if someone is all right

Are you OK?

Are you all right?

Are you feeling OK?

Life got you down? (*informal*)

Are things getting you down?

You look like you lost your best friend. (*cliché*)

You look like the wind has been taken out of your sails. (*idiomatic*)

What's the matter?
Something got you down?
What's got you down?
Why are you so blue?

 blue = sad

Why is your face so long?

 face so long = face so sad

Who rained on your parade? (*idiomatic*)

 rained on your parade = ruined your plans

What rained on your parade? (*idiomatic*)
Did someone rain on your parade? (*idiomatic*)
Who burst your bubble? (*idiomatic*)

 = *Who ruined your good outlook on life?*

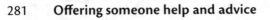

281   **Offering someone help and advice**

Would you like to talk about it?
Need someone to talk to?
If you need someone to talk to, I'm always available.
I'm here if you want to talk about it.

282   **Encouraging someone who is unhappy**

Cheer up!
Things are never as bad as they seem.
It will (all) work out.
Don't let it get you down. (*idiomatic*)
Chin up. (*cliché*)
Keep your chin up. (*cliché*)
Things will get better.
Tomorrow is another day. (*cliché*)
It's always darkest before dawn. (*cliché*)

Stop carrying the weight of the world on your shoulders.

There's no point in carrying the weight of the world on your shoulders.

283   When you are depressed

I'm depressed.

> *I'm = He's, She's, They're, We're, Tom's, Janet's, etc.*

I'm feeling low.

I'm feeling down.

I'm feeling blue. (*idiomatic*)

> *blue = sad*

I'm out of sorts.

I'm in the doldrums.

I'm a little down in the mouth. (*idiomatic*)

I'm down in the dumps.

> *= I am depressed.*

I've been down in the dumps lately.

I can't put my finger on what's wrong.

284   Expressing despair and emptiness

My heart is heavy.

> *My = Her, His, Our, Janet's, Tom's, etc.*

My heart is broken.

I'm downhearted.

> *I'm = He's, She's, They're, We're, Tom's, Janet's, etc.*

I'm broken-hearted.

I'm heartbroken.

285   When someone looks very happy

You look like you just won the jackpot.

You look like you died and went to heaven.

You're looking on top of the world.
What're you smiling about?

286   When someone is very happy—idioms

I'm on Cloud Nine.
> *I'm = He's, She's, They're, We're, Tom's, Jane's, etc.*

I'm in seventh heaven.
I'm walking on air.
I'm on top of the world.
I'm sitting on top of the world.
I'm high on life.
I'm feeling good.
I'm feeling fine.
I'm as merry as the day is long.
I'm happy as can be.
I'm happy as a clam.
I'm as happy as a clam.
I'm as pleased as punch.
I'm beside myself with joy.
I couldn't be happier.

287   Expressing enthusiasm for life

Things couldn't be better.
Everything's coming up roses.
I don't have a care in the world.
What a great day!
It's great to be alive!
It feels good just to be alive!
Life's been good to me.

288   When someone is content

My mind's at ease.
I'm content.

We're satisfied.

I'm just going with the flow.

He's as snug as a bug in a rug.

I'm at peace. (*formal*)

289 When someone is carefree

I'm footloose and fancy-free. (*cliché*)

I don't have a care in the world.

Tom is without a care in the world.

I haven't a care.

290 When someone is resigned to life as it is

I accept myself for what I am.

I've come to terms with myself.

I've come to terms with reality.

I've come to grips with reality.

I've learned to face the music. (*idiomatic*)

> *to face the music = to face life; to face reality*

Leave well enough alone. (*cliché*)

Let well enough alone.

Let sleeping dogs lie. (*cliché*)

> = *Do not try to solve a problem that is not causing extreme difficulties at the moment.*

I accept myself for what I am.

I've learned to face the music.

291 Expressing displeasure with something

That leaves a lot to be desired.

That's not what I had in mind.

That didn't fit the bill.

> *to fit the bill = to be what is needed*

That doesn't quite suit me.

It's not up to snuff.

> *up to snuff = up to standard*

That's not what it's cracked up to be.

    cracked up to be = said to be

292   Asking someone to stop being unpleasant

Stop griping.
Stop complaining.
Quit complaining.
Quit whining.
Quit your bitching. (*mildly vulgar*)
Quit your kvetching. (*informal*)

    kvetching = complaining

Quit your beefing. (*slang*)

    to beef = to complain

Quit your bellyaching. (*slang*)

    to bellyache = to complain

Don't be such a grouch.
Don't be such a crab.

    a crab = a crabby person = a grouchy person

Don't be so grouchy.
Don't be so grumpy.

    grumpy = irritable; out of sorts

Did you get up on the wrong side of the bed? (*idiomatic*)
Somebody didn't get enough sleep.
Stop sulking.
Stop pouting.

293   Dullness and boredom

I'm bored.
I'm bored to tears.
I'm bored to death.
I'm bored to distraction.
I'm bored stiff.
I'm bored silly.

Ho-hum.

Are we having fun yet?

When does the fun start?

That went over like a lead balloon. (*idiomatic*)

That was a flop.

    a flop = a failure

That flopped.

What a yawner.

    a yawner = something boring that causes yawns

He is as dull as dishwater. (*cliché*)

This is like watching paint dry.

He could go on forever.

He's like a broken record.

She really wears on me.

Wake me up when it's over.

I'm sick and tired of this.

I'm fed up.

I need a change of scenery.

I need a change of pace.

294   Dullness in people

Must you harp on the same string?

Must you keep harping on that?

Must you dwell on the subject?

Must you beat a dead horse?

Don't be such a stick-in-the-mud.

Don't be such a party pooper. (*jocular*)

    a party pooper = a dull person who ruins parties

Don't be such a wet blanket. (*informal*)

    a wet blanket = someone who ruins all the fun, as a wet blanket
        smothers a fire

Don't be such a killjoy. (*informal*)

    a killjoy = someone who ruins all the fun

295   Excitement in people

She's the life of the party.
He's (such) a card.
He's a kill. (*slang*)

Anxiety

296   When you feel out of place

I was in the wrong place at the wrong time.
I feel like a fish out of water.
I'm out of my element.
When in Rome, do as the Romans do. (*cliché*)
When in Rome. (*informal*)

297   Expressing anger

I'm so furious.
I'm so mad I could scream.
I've never been so mad in my life.
I was chewing nails.
Tom was loaded for bear.
She was shooting daggers at me.
If looks could kill . . .

298   Expressing fright

I was scared.
I was frightened.
I was terrified.
I was petrified.
I was scared to death.
I was scared silly.

You scared me.

You frightened me.

You scared the hell out of me. (*mildly vulgar*)

You scared the crap out of me. (*mildly vulgar*)

You scared the dickens out of me.

You scared the devil out of me.

You scared the wits out of me.

You scared me out of my wits.

You scared me to death.

You scared me half to death.

You scared the daylights out of me.

You scared the living daylights out of me.

You scared the pants off me. (*informal*)

I almost jumped out of my skin.

I almost lost it.

It gave me the creeps. (*slang*)

It gave me the willies. (*slang*)

It made my flesh crawl.

It gave me goose bumps.

It gave me goose pimples.

A shiver ran down my spine.

It curled my hair.

My hair stood on end.

My blood ran cold.

My blood curdled.

It set my teeth on edge.

299   When you do not know what to say

I'm at a loss for words.

I'm speechless.

I'm dumbstruck.

No comment.

I have no response.

I have nothing to say.

I have nothing to add.

I don't know what to say.

What can I say?

What do you want me to say?

You got me there.

The Senses

300   Difficulty in hearing

I'm sorry, I'm hard of hearing.

I'm sorry, I'm hearing-impaired.

He suffered a hearing loss.

He's stone deaf.

> *stone = completely*

She's deaf as a post. (*informal*)

301   An ear for music

I don't have an ear for music.

I'm tone-deaf.

He's got an ear for the piano.

She plays piano by ear.

302   Hearing loud and soft sounds

I can't hear them; they're out of earshot.

It was so quiet you could hear a pin drop.

That noise is deafening.

That noise assaults the ear. (*formal*)

That noise is setting my teeth on edge.

What a racket!

> *racket = noise*

Are you trying to wake the dead?

My ears are ringing.

303   Concerning ears or hearing

My plea fell on deaf ears. (*cliché*)

They turned a deaf ear to our plea. (*idiomatic*)

There's none so deaf as those who will not hear. (*cliché*)

In one ear and out the other. (*cliché*)

To hear tell, the whole situation was awful.

Boy, did I get an earful.

     an earful = a long explanation; a scolding

Prick up your ears! (*idiomatic*)

Keep your ears open.

Hear no evil. (*cliché*)

304   The taste of foods

Delicious.

That tastes great.

Tastes great.

That's as sweet as honey.

That's as sweet as sugar.

That tastes terrible.

That tastes like chicken.

That turns my stomach.

That's unfit for human consumption.

305   Offering someone a small portion of food

Would you like a taste?

Here. Try some.

Would you like a sip?

306   Expressing hunger

I'm hungry.

I'm famished.

I'm starved.

I'm ravenous.

My mouth is watering.

That stew is mouthwatering.

I'm so hungry I could eat a horse. (*cliché*)

I could eat a horse. (*cliché*)

307   Identifying smells

What's that smell?

What smells?

Do you smell something?

What's that fragrance?

What's that aroma?

What's that scent?

What's that odor?

What's that stench?

What stinks? (*informal*)

Do you smell gas?

Get a whiff of this!

Take a whiff of this.

Sniff this.

That reeks.

That smells.

That smells to high heaven!

That stinks to high heaven! (*informal*)

It stinks on ice. (*slang*)

308   Physical responses

That sends shivers down my spine.

It gave me goose bumps.

It gave me the chills.

It gave me butterflies in my stomach. (*idiomatic*)

309 The sense of touch

It was (as) soft as silk.
It was (as) hard as a rock.
It was (as) hard as stone.
The fish felt slimy.

310 Difficulties with seeing

I'm as blind as a bat. (*cliché*)
I can't see a thing without my glasses.
I can't quite make it out.

311 Concerning good vision

I have good eyesight.
I have excellent vision.
I have 20/20 vision.
I've got a good eye for color.
I've got an eye for composition.

312 Concerning vision and belief

I can't believe my eyes.
My eyes betray me. (*formal*)
Do my eyes deceive me?
There's none so blind as those who will not see. (*cliché*)

Health and Appearance

313 When someone is in good health

His doctor gave him a clean bill of health.
    a clean bill of health = a good report on one's health

He's the picture of health.
He's in the pink.
He looks great.
He's looking good.
He's in top form.
He's at the top of his form.
I couldn't be better.
I feel like a million dollars.
I feel like a million bucks.
She looks like a million dollars.
She looks like a million bucks.
He's bright-eyed and bushy-tailed. (*idiomatic*)
I'm sound as a dollar. (*cliché*)
I'm fresh as a daisy. (*cliché*)
She's healthy as a horse. (*cliché*)
She's fit as a fiddle. (*cliché*)

314 Observing that someone looks disorderly

You look tired.
You look like you need some sleep.
You look dreadful.
You look terrible.
You look like hell. (*mildly vulgar*)
You look a sight.
You're a sight.
Look what the cat dragged in. (*informal*)
You look like something the cat dragged in. (*informal*)
You look like you've been to hell and back. (*informal*)
You look like you've been through a war.
You look like you've gone through the wringer.

315 When someone looks very bad

You could stop a truck. (*informal*)
You could stop a clock. (*informal*)

That face could stop a clock. (*informal*)
Are you having a bad hair day? (*informal*)
You're as ugly as sin. (*informal*)

316   Inquiring about someone's health or well-being

Are you OK?
Are you feeling OK?
Are you all right?
Do you feel all right?

317   When someone does not look well

You don't look well.
You don't look too good. (*informal*)
You don't look so good. (*informal*)
You look like death.
You look like death warmed over.
You look green around the gills.
You look a little peaked.
You look flushed.
You look pale.
You're pale.
You're white as a ghost.

Sickness

318   Concerning allergies

I'm allergic to sulfa.
> *I'm allergic to = I have an allergy to, I can't tolerate*
I'm allergic to penicillin.
I'm allergic to cats.

I'm allergic to dogs.
I'm allergic to pollen.
I'm allergic to dust.
I'm allergic to bees.
I'm allergic to bee stings.
I'm allergic to chocolate.
I'm allergic to nuts.
I'm allergic to shrimp.
I'm allergic to strawberries.
I can't have chocolate.
I can't eat strawberries.
I can't drink milk.
I can't have dairy products.
I can't digest milk.
I'm lactose intolerant.
I'm on a gluten-free diet.
I have hay fever.
Dairy products make me break out in a rash.
My ID bracelet lists my allergies.
   ID = *identification*
I have an environmental illness.

319   Allergic problems with the nose and breathing

My allergies are acting up.
My sinuses are acting up.
My sinuses are bothering me.
My sinuses are congested.
My sinuses ache.
My nose is clogged.
My nose is stuffed up.
My nose is congested.
I can't breathe.

320   When someone sneezes

Bless you.
God bless you.
Gesundheit. (*German*)

321   Allergic problems with the eyes

My eyes are swollen.
My eyes are puffy.
My eyes itch.
My eyes are itchy.

322   Allergic problems with the skin

My skin is breaking out.
I'm breaking out.
I'm breaking out in hives.
I break out when I eat chocolate.
My skin itches whenever I eat shrimp.

323   Expressing general feelings of illness

I'm sick.
I feel sick.
I'm sick as a dog. (*informal*)
I feel funny.
I feel awful.
I feel downright awful.
I feel terrible.
I feel lousy.
I feel rotten.
I feel like hell. (*mildly vulgar*)

I don't feel well.
I don't feel so well.
I don't feel quite right.
I feel ill.
I'm not feeling myself.
I'm feeling under the weather.
I'm a little under the weather.
I'm feeling a little down in the mouth.

325   When you feel like vomiting

I feel sick to my stomach.
I'm sick to my stomach.
I feel nauseous.
I feel like throwing up. (*informal*)
I think I'm going to throw up. (*informal*)
I think I'm going to vomit.
I'm going to barf. (*slang*)
    to barf = to vomit
I think I'm going to be sick.
    to lose my lunch = to vomit

326   Describing a pain in the head

I have a headache.
My head hurts.
My head is killing me.
I've got a splitting headache.
My head is throbbing.
My head is pounding.
There's a hammering inside my head.
I have a migraine.
I have an excruciating headache.

327 Describing dizziness

I'm dizzy.

The room is spinning.

I'm so dizzy I can't stand up.

I'm so dizzy I have to sit down.

328 Describing being exhausted or worn out

I'm exhausted.

I need some rest.

I need a nap.

I need to take a day off.

I need a day off.

I need a vacation.

My get-up-and-go has got up and left. (*informal*)

> *get-up-and-go = energy; vitality*

I'm exhausted!

I need to take a day off.

329 Offering care to a sick person

Can I get you a glass of water?

Do you want a glass of water?

Would you like a glass of water?

Would a glass of water help?

Would you like to lie down?

Want to lie down?

Would you like some aspirin?

> *aspirin = Tylenol, Advil, ibuprofen, etc.*

Want some aspirin?

Should I call a doctor?

Have you seen a doctor?

330 Concerning catching a disease

Is it catching?

Are you contagious?

Don't give it to me.
I don't want to catch it.
You need to relax.
You've been running around too much.
Your resistance is down.
It's been going around.

331 Questions for the hospital patient

Have they figured out what's wrong?
What's the prognosis?
  the prognosis = the prediction for the future outcome of an illness
How long will you be here?
When do you get to go home?
When are you going home?
When are you being released?
Is there anything you need?
Do you need anything?
Is there anything I can do?
Can I get you anything?
Should I call for the nurse?
Is the food as bad as they say?
How's the food?
How's your doctor?

332 Explaining that your health is improving

I'm improving.
I'm getting better.
I'm getting over it.
I'm getting back on my feet.
I'm getting back on my legs.
I'm getting back to normal.
I'm bouncing back.
I'm on the road to recovery.
I'm out of the woods.

Things are looking up.
I've hit bottom and things are looking up.
I'm better now.
I'm better than I was.

333 Explaining that you are receiving medical care

I still have to go back to the doctor for a follow-up.
I'm still under a doctor's care.
I'm still seeing a doctor.
I'm in therapy.
I'm still seeing a therapist.

334 Explaining that you are cured of a health problem

I'm well now.
I'm all better.
I'm completely over it.
I'm as good as new.
It's like it never happened.
I feel like a new person.
I've got a new lease on life.

FAMILY MATTERS

Home Life

335 Describing family relationships

You're just like your mother.
You take after your father.
You are your father all over again.

It's like I'm talking to your mother.

She looks just like her mother.

She looks just like her mother did at that age.

She's the picture of her mother.

She favors her mother.

He's the spit and image of his grandfather.

He's the spitting image of his grandfather.

He's got his father's features.

She's got her mother's nose.

   = *Her nose is very much like her mother's nose.*

She resembles her Aunt Martha.

He's a chip off the old block.

She's following in her father's footsteps.

Like father, like son.

Like mother, like daughter.

He's a real mama's boy.

She's a real daddy's girl.

She's daddy's little girl.

336   **Family solidarity**

We are (all) family.

Blood runs thicker than water.

How can you do that to your own flesh and blood?

The family that prays together stays together. (*cliché*)

337   **Asking about a meal**

When do we eat?

What's to eat?

What's for supper?

What are we having?

338   Announcing a meal

Dinner's almost ready.
It's almost done.
It will be on the table in a minute.
It's almost ready.
(It's) time to eat.
Dinner's ready.
Soup's on! (*informal*)
    = *Dinner's ready!*

339   Instructions given to children in the kitchen

Don't sit on the counter.
Don't eat that; you'll spoil your dinner.
Don't stand in front of the refrigerator with the door open.
Watch out; it's hot!
Don't drink milk out of the carton!
Don't drink milk out of the jug!
Would you set the table?
Go sit down; supper's ready.
Go tell your father supper's ready.
Call the family to dinner.
Call everyone to the table.

340   Blessing the food

Sarah, would you say grace?
Who wants to say grace?
Fold your hands.

341   Second servings

Could you pour me some more milk?
More milk, please.
A drop more wine, please.

Could I have seconds, please?
May I have seconds, please?
Would you like some more of this?
Is there any more of this?
What's for dessert?

342 Instructing children on good table manners

Don't put your elbows on the table.
Don't talk with your mouth full.
Don't read at the table.
No TV during dinner.

  TV = television

Wipe your mouth.
Put your napkin on your lap.
Put your napkin in your lap.

343 Doing the dishes

Andrew, please clear the table.
Please put your dishes in the sink.

  dishes = all crockery and utensils

Please carry your own dishes to the kitchen.
It's your turn to do the dishes.
It's your turn to clear the table.
I'll scrape and you load (the dishwasher).
Whose turn is it to do the dishes?
I'll wash and you dry.

344 Asking to leave the dinner table early

May I please leave the table?
  (said by a child)
May I be excused?
  (said by a child)

Do you mind if I leave the table?
  (said by an adult)
I'll have to excuse myself.
  (said by an adult)
Would you excuse me?

345 Instructing children to finish eating

Finish your dinner.
You have to eat everything.
You have to eat everything that you serve yourself.
You have to eat some of everything.
You have to clean up your plate.
If you don't eat your vegetables, you won't get any dessert.
If you don't eat your dinner, you won't get any dessert.
There are starving children in Africa.
  Africa = Bosnia, Asia, South America, etc.

346 Concerning a radio or stereo

Turn the stereo down.
Turn the stereo off.
Turn the radio off.
Let's find a different station.
What station is this?
What do you want to hear?

347 Concerning furniture or carpeting

Don't wear your shoes on the good carpet.
Don't sit on the good furniture.
Don't put your feet on the furniture.
Keep your feet off (of) the furniture.

348   Concerning television

What's on TV?

    TV = television

What's on?

What's on tonight?

What's on the tube?

    the tube = the television (picture tube)

What's on channel five?

What do you want to watch?

What do you want to see?

What are you watching?

Where is the TV guide?

Where is the TV listing?

Is this any good?

Is there anything on?

There anything good on?

349   Changing the television channel

Find a channel and stick with it. (*informal*)

Stick with one channel. (*informal*)

Stick to one channel. (*informal*)

Stop flipping channels. (*informal*)

Change the channel.

Let's change the channel.

Hand me the remote control.

Where is the remote (control)?

Give me the remote.

350   Managing a television set

You're sitting too close to the TV.

Can't you get a better picture?

Turn the TV off if you're not watching it.

Turn it up, please.

Please adjust the rabbit ears.

>   *rabbit ears = a type of indoor television antenna*

Please adjust the antenna.

Turn it down.

Could you please turn it down?

Please turn down the TV.

Turn it off.

351   Concerning computers

You're always on the computer.

Are you on Facebook?

>   *Facebook = MySpace, Twitter, LinkedIn, etc.*

I need to check my e-mail.

>   *e-mail = Facebook, Ebay account, etc.*

I need to send an e-mail.

Look it up online.

I looked it up on Google.

>   *Google = Yahoo, Wikipedia, etc.*

I googled it. (*informal*)

Did you see that funny video online?

It's up on YouTube.

I'll send you the link.

I need to send an e-mail.

Did you see that funny video online?

352   Managing a computer

What's your log-on?

What's the password?

I've forgotten the password.

Remember to log off.

My files are on my laptop.

>   *laptop = computer, notebook, flash drive, etc.*

I put all my photos up online.

>   *online = on Flickr, on Shutterfly, etc.*

I've uploaded all my videos.

Back up your files.
Do you have a flash drive?

353 Taking a nap

I'm going to take a nap.
I'm going to take a catnap.
> *a catnap = a short nap*

I'm going to take a snooze.
> *a snooze = a nap*

I'm going to get some shut-eye.
> *some shut-eye = some sleep*

I'm going to catch forty winks.
> *forty winks = some sleep*

I'm going to catch some Zs.
> *Zs = snoring = sleep*

354 Going to bed and to sleep

I'm off to bed.
I'm going to bed.
It's bedtime.
It's past my bedtime.
I'm going to sleep.
I'm going to hit the sack. (*idiomatic*)
I'm going to hit the hay. (*idiomatic*)
I'm going to crash. (*slang*)
I think I'll retire for the night. (*formal*)
I think I'll say good night now.

355 Saying good night

Good night.
Sleep tight. Don't let the bedbugs bite.
> (*usually said to a child*)

See you in the morning.

Sweet dreams.

Pleasant dreams.

Sleep well.

Night-night.

    (usually said to a child)

Nighty-night.

    (usually said to a child)

356   Commands for a dog

Sit.

Stay.

Roll over.

Shake hands.

Shake.

Play dead.

Fetch!

Heel.

Sic 'em.

    sic = attack

Come!

Come here.

Here, boy!

Here, girl!

Good boy!

Good girl!

Bad dog!

Do you want to go outside?

357   Caring for pets

Did you walk the dog?

Someone has to walk the dog.

Will you please put the cat out?

The dog wants to get out.

Where is the gerbil?

The guinea pig is loose again.

Please clean the (cat's) litter (box) now!

The cat's litter needs changing.

We're out of dog chow.

> *dog chow = dried dog food*

Education

358   Getting ready to study or do homework

Time to crack the books.

> *to crack = to open*

Time to hit the books.

> *to hit = to use*

Gotta cram. (*slang*)

> *to cram = to study hard; to cram knowledge into one's brain*

I need to cram for a final. (*slang*)

I need to prep for a big test. (*slang*)

I have a lot of studying to do.

I have to study.

I've got to study.

I've got a midterm tomorrow.

I've got a final exam tomorrow.

I've got a big test tomorrow.

I've got a big exam tomorrow.

359   Talking to a child's teacher

I'd like to discuss my daughter's progress.

I'd like to talk about my daughter's grade.

How is my daughter doing in class?

My daughter seems to be having trouble in class.
She's having a hard time with her homework.
What can I do to help her at home?
How can I help her with her homework?

360 Returning to school after an absence

Do you have a note from home?
Do you have a note from
your mother?
Do you have a note from
your doctor?

361 Questioning a college professor

Can I still get into your course?
What texts are required?
What is the book list for
the course?
Is a paper required for this course?
Is there a final for this course?
Is attendance required in this course?
What are the requirements?
When are your office hours?
Where is your office?

362 Asking for clarification in a college classroom

Could you explain that again?
I don't get it. Please explain.
Please go over that part again.
I don't understand.
I still don't understand.
I do not understand your English. Please speak more plainly.
I'm having a problem understanding the TA.
    TA = Teaching Assistant

363   Asking about classroom examinations

When is the final (exam)?

When is the midterm?

What do you want us to know for the test?

What will the test cover?

Will there be a review session?

Will the test cover the whole book?

Will the test take the whole period?

What's on the test?

364   Asking about a classroom assignment

How many pages do we have to read for Monday?

How many pages?

Will we have to turn in our homework?

What's the reading assignment for next time?

Will there be a quiz?

What's the assignment for tomorrow?

When is the assignment due?

365   Asking about grades

Can you tell me what grade I'm getting?

Would you tell me what grade I'm getting?

Do you grade on a curve?

How many As were there?

What's the grading curve?

I worked hard, so don't I deserve
a good grade?

Can I talk to you about my grade?

366   Meeting children

And how are you today?
And what is your name?
How old are you?

367   Concerning a child's growth and development

You're turning into quite a little lady!

You've gotten so big!
You're growing so tall.
You're turning into (quite) a little lady.
You're turning into (quite) a little gentleman.
What a big girl!
My, my! Haven't you grown!

368   Posing questions to children

What grade are you in?
How do you like school?
Do you go to school yet?
How many years till you're in school?
What's your favorite subject in school?
Have you been a good boy?
Are you being a good girl?
How many brothers and sisters do you have?

369   Praising a small child

That's very good.
You're a good little boy.
You're a good little girl.
Good boy!
Good girl!

Big boy!
What a big girl!
I'm so proud of you.
Mommy's proud of you.
We are very proud of you.

370   Scolding a child

Behave.
Behave yourself.
Be good.
Be a good girl.
Be a good boy.
That's enough of that!

371   Encouraging a child to be quiet

Sit down.
Be quiet.
Quiet!
Let's be quiet.
Shhh!
Hush!
Not another word!
I don't want to hear a(nother) peep out of you!
   a peep = a sound

I don't want to hear a single peep out of you!

372   Asking a child to stop some behavior

Stop it.
Stop that.
Settle down.
That's enough of that!
Simmer down.

373   Asking a child to leave things alone

Put that down.

Keep your hands to yourself.

Look with your eyes not your hands. (*cliché*)

Put that away.

Leave that alone.

Don't touch that.

Stop playing with that.

374   Asking a child to leave people alone

Don't bother your father while he's driving.

Stop pestering your little brother.

Keep your hands to yourself.

Keep your hands off your little brother.

Stop teasing your little sister.

Leave him alone.

Leave him be.

Let him be.

375   Making sure a child understands

Do as I say.

Do as I say, not as I do.

Do as I tell you.

Do what I tell you.

Do as you're told.

Do you understand?

Understand?

Is that clear?

Have I made myself clear?

Do I make myself clear?

Do I make myself perfectly clear?

Did you hear me?

Do you hear me?

Do you hear?

376 Concerning a child's use of good manners

Mind your manners.

Mind your Ps and Qs. (*idiomatic*)

Behave.

Behave yourself.

I expect you to be on your best behavior.

Act like a lady.

Act like a gentleman.

Say "excuse me."

Say "thank you."

Say "you're welcome."

Say "please."

What's the magic word?

> *the magic word = the word* please

What do you say?

> = *Say* "please."

Yes, what?

> = *Say* "Yes, sir; Yes, ma'am; or Yes, please."

(Always) remember to say please and thank you.

FOOD AND DRINK

Restaurants

377 Asking for a table at a restaurant

A table for one.

A table for two.

Two, please.

I would like a nonsmoking table for two.

I have a reservation.

378 Concerning seating in a restaurant

Your waiter will be Alfredo.

Enjoy your meal.

Would you like smoking or nonsmoking?

Smoking or nonsmoking?

Smoking or non?

Do you have a reservation?

How many in your party?

Table for four?

Party of four?

> *party = group*

Four?

We'll have a table ready in just a few minutes.

It'll be just a few minutes.

There's a ten-minute wait.

We have a table ready for Smith, party of four.

Table for Smith, party of four.

Smith, party of four.

Your waiter will be Alfredo.

Enjoy your meal. (*cliché*)

Enjoy. (*informal*)

379 Concerning smoking in a restaurant

Is this a nonsmoking restaurant?

Do you have a nonsmoking section?

I'd like the smoking section.

I'd like the nonsmoking section.

Please seat me as far as possible from the smoking section.

Smoking.

Nonsmoking.

380 Explaining that someone else will join you at a restaurant

Another party will be sitting here.
We are waiting for another couple.
My friend will be along shortly.
I am expecting someone else.
I'm waiting for someone else.

381 Greetings from a waiter or waitress

Hello.
Sorry to keep you waiting.
How are you today?
My name's Sandy. I'll be your waitress this evening.
My name's Sandy. I'll be your server this evening.
I'm Bobby. I'm your server.

382 Questions a waiter or waitress might ask

Are you waiting for someone?
Will someone be joining you?
Good evening, would you care for a drink?
Would you like to start with a cocktail?
Would you like something to drink first?
Would you like to order a drink?
Can I get you something to drink?
Would anyone like coffee?
Coffee?
Cream or sugar?
Would you like to see a menu?
Would you care to see the wine list?
Are you ready to order?
Do you need a few more minutes (to decide what you want)?
Would you like to see the menu again for dessert?

383 Reciting special meal offers for the day

Let me tell you about our specials today.

The special of the day is roast beef and brown gravy with potatoes and two vegetables.

The specials are listed on the board.

The specials are on the right side (of the menu).

384 When a restaurant is out of some item

I'm sorry, we're out of that.

Sorry, it's all gone.

The chef informs me we're out of that. (*formal*)

385 Questions asked of a restaurant customer

Would you like soup or salad with that?

How would you like that prepared?

How would you like your steak prepared?

How would you like your steak?

How would you like that done?

How would you like that?

What kind of potatoes would you like?

Mashed, boiled, hash browns, or French fries?

Would you like a baked potato, fries, or rice?

That comes with a salad.

Would you like soup or salad with that?

Soup or salad?

The soup of the day is split pea or chicken noodle.

Our dressings are Ranch, Italian, Thousand Island, Greek, and house.

> *house = the standard dressing used in this restaurant*

Would you like some fresh ground pepper?

Say when.

> = *Speak when you have had enough.*

386   Requesting something to drink at a restaurant

Coffee, please.
I'd like some coffee.
I'd like some decaf.
    decaf = decaffeinated coffee

I'd like an espresso.
I'd like tea.
Just coffee for the moment.
Just coffee for now.
Black coffee.
Coffee with cream.
Cream and sugar.
Can you get me a glass of water?
Could we have some water, please?

387   Requesting attention from a waiter or waitress

Can you come here when you have a second?
Oh, waiter!
Oh, miss!
Excuse me, ma'am.
Pardon me.
Excuse me.

388   Explaining to a waiter or waitress that you are not ready to order

We need a couple more minutes to decide.
I need a few more minutes to decide.
Could I see a menu, please?
I'm not ready to order yet.
I haven't figured out what I want yet.
I haven't decided yet.

389   Indicating readiness to order a meal at a restaurant

We're ready to order.
Can we order now?
Can you take our orders now?
We're ready.

390   Asking about specific items on a restaurant menu

What are the specials?
What is the special of the day?
Do you have any specials?
What would you suggest?
Do you have any recommendations?
What's good today?
What does that come with?
What comes with that?
Does that come with a salad?
What kind of dressing do you have?
Do you have any lo-cal dressing?
    lo-cal = low calorie
What's the soup of the day?
Is that prepared with meat?
Is there meat in that?
Do you have vegetarian dishes?

391   Requesting that certain foods not be served to you in a restaurant

No mayo(nnaise), please.
    mayo(nnaise) = nuts, onions, garlic, lettuce, bacon, pickles, etc.
No mayo.
Hold the mayo.
Leave off the mayo.

I'd like that without MSG, please.

    MSG = monosodium glutamate, typically used in Chinese food

Does this contain MSG?

Does this contain nuts?

I cannot tolerate nuts. I'm allergic.

No nuts. I'm allergic.

No MSG, please.

I'm allergic to dairy products.

I'm allergic to wheat.

393   Telling how a steak is to be cooked in a restaurant

I'd like my steak well done.

    well done = completely cooked

I'd like my steak rare.

    rare = partially cooked

I'd like my steak medium.

    medium = between rare and well done

Please make sure it's well-done.

I'd like my steak medium-well.

I want the steak thoroughly cooked.

I'd like my steak medium-rare.

Can I get it rare?

I'd like my steak medium-rare, please.

394   Requesting additional servings in a restaurant

I need more coffee.

Could I have more coffee, please?

Could I have some more bread, please?

Could I have some more water, please?

More bread, please. (*informal*)

Could I have some more butter?

395   Ordering wine in a restaurant

May I see the wine list?
Could I see your wine list?
I'd like a glass of wine.
I'd like a carafe of wine.
We'd like to order a bottle of wine.

This is cold. Can you take it back to the kitchen?

396   Making a complaint in a restaurant

I can't eat this.
This meat is too fatty.
This meat is too tough.
This meat isn't fresh.
This fish isn't fresh.
I didn't order this.
These vegetables are hardly cooked at all.
The vegetables are overcooked and mushy.
This is cold. Can you take it back to the kitchen?
Could I speak with the manager, please?

397   Asking about the location of a restroom in a public building

Is there somewhere I could wash my hands?
Where are the public restrooms?
Where is the washroom?
Where is the men's room?
Where is the ladies' room?
Where would I find the restrooms?
Where's the john? (*informal*)
    the john = the toilet; a restroom

398   Ordering food to be taken out

Do you have carryout?
I would like to order something to carry out.

Can I get that to go?

To go, please.

399 Requests to have uneaten food wrapped so it can be taken home

Could you wrap this, please?

Could we have a doggie bag?

> a doggie bag = a special bag or container for taking uneaten food
> home from a restaurant (as if it were being taken home to feed the
> dog)

I'd like to take the rest.

I'd like to take the rest home.

400 When your food is brought to the table in a restaurant

Here's your order.

There you go.

Careful, the plate is hot.

Enjoy your meal.

Enjoy. (*informal*)

401 Asking for a diner's opinion of a meal

I hope that everything is satisfactory.

Is everything all right?

Is everything OK?

How are you doing?

Are you enjoying your meal?

How's your steak?

How's that steak?

402 A waiter or waitress seeking to be of further service

More coffee?

Is there anything I can get for you?

Is there anything I can get you?

Is there anything else?
Is there anything else I can get for you this evening? (*formal*)
Is there anything else I can get for you?
Anything else I can do for you?

403   A waiter or waitress offering dessert

Would you care for dessert?
Would you like to try one of our desserts?
Would you like to see the dessert menu?
Would you like to see the menu again?
Let me show you the dessert tray.

404   Asking for the bill in a restaurant

Could I have the bill?
Could I have the check?
We'd like the bill, please.
Check, please.
Separate checks, please.
Do I pay you or the cashier?
Do you take this (credit card)?
Can I have a receipt, please?
May I have a receipt, please? (*formal*)
We are ready to leave now.
All together.
All on one (check).

405   About payment for a meal in a restaurant

Is this all on one bill?
Separate checks?
You can pay at the register.
You can pay me.
I'll take it when you're ready.

406   Concerning the payment of a bill in a restaurant

There seems to be a mistake.
We did not order this item.
Does this include the tip?
Does this include a gratuity?
Is a gratuity included?
Keep the change.

Bars

407   A bartender asking what you want

What's yours?
What'll you have?
May I help you?
What'll it be, friend? (*informal*)
Another (of the same)?

408   Asking what's available at a bar

What (beer) do you have on tap?
> *on tap = ready to be drawn from a keg*

What kind of beer do you have?
What beers ya got? (*informal*)
What (beer) do you have on draft?
> *on draft = ready to be drawn from a keg*

What kinds of wine do you have?
Do you have any imported beer?

409   Requesting a glass or bottle of beer

I'll have a beer.

> *I'll have = Please give me, Give me, I'll take, Make mine, Gimme,*
> *Do you have (?)*

I'll have a Bud.

> *Bud = Miller's, Budweiser, Heineken, Mich(elob), Special Export,*
> *Coors, etc.*

I'll have a draft.

> *a draft = a beer drawn from a keg, or a bottle of beer with "Draft" in*
> *the brand name*

Make it a cold one.

> *a cold one = a cold beer*

Pour me a beer. (*informal*)

Give me a beer. (*informal*)

410   Various requests for drinks from a bartender

I'd like (some) coffee.

> *I'd like = Can I please have (?), I'll take, Please get me*

I'd like (some) coffee with cream.

I'd like (some) coffee with sugar.

I'd like (some) coffee with cream and sugar.

I'd like a Coke.

I'd like some Coke.

I'd like a diet cola.

I'd like a mineral water.

I'd like a beer.

I'd like a glass of beer.

I'd like a stein of beer.

I'd like a pitcher of beer.

I'd like a light beer.

I'd like a dark beer.

I'd like a domestic beer.

I'd like a draft beer.

I'd like an ale.

I'd like a lager.

I'd like a glass of wine.

I'd like some champagne.

I'd like a scotch.

I'd like a scotch on the rocks.

I'd like a whiskey with soda.

I'd like a gin and tonic.

I'd like a gin and tonic with a twist.

411   Special instructions to a bartender

Make it dry.

> = I prefer a dry Martini or a dry wine.

Hold the cherry.

Give me another.

I'll have another (one) of the same.

> the same = the same as previously ordered

I'll have the same.

Two olives, please.

I'd like it on the rocks.

> on the rocks = with ice cubes

Make that on the rocks.

412   Buying drinks with friends

I'm buying.

Let me get this (one).

It's on me.

> on me = on my account = I'm paying

The next round is on me.

> round = an order of drinks for everyone

No, no, this one's on me!

This is my round.

This round's on me.

It's on me.
I'm buying.
Who's buying?
Want to run a tab?

> *a tab = a running account*

413 Charges for drinks at a bar

That'll be six bucks.
Do you wish to pay me now?
Would you like to start a tab?
You've run up quite a tab.
You really have to pay something
   von your bill.

414 Expressions used with friends at a bar asking about drinks

What are we having?
Do you all want to get a pitcher?
Anyone for a pizza?
Name your poison.
What'll you have?
What's yours?
Care for another?

What are we having?

Name your poison.

415 Expressions about drinking additional drinks

I'm going to drown my sorrows.
Let's have another round.
Let's have a nightcap.

> *a nightcap = a final drink of the evening*

Let's knock back another.
Let's toss one back.

I'll have just a nip.

 a nip = a swallow

I'll have just a sip.

I'll have a shot.

 a shot = a swallow; a jigger

Give me a swig.

 a swig = a swallow

Give me a hit.

 a hit = a swallow

Give me a jigger.

 a jigger = 1.5 ounces; a 1.5-ounce glass

Give me
a swig.

417   **Encouraging someone to drink**

That'll put hair on your chest. (*idiomatic*)

 = The drink is strong, and it will invigorate you.

Let's tie one on. (*slang*)

 = Let's get drunk.

That'll knock your socks off. (*idiomatic*)

 = The drink is very strong, and it will shock your system.

This'll wet your whistle. (*idiomatic*)

 = This drink will quench your thirst.

Let's get down to some serious drinking. (*informal*)

 = Let's get drunk together.

Have a hair of the dog that bit you. (*cliché*)

 = Have some more of what made you drunk.

Let's paint the town red. (*cliché*)

 = Let's celebrate.

Party down! (*slang*)

Party hearty! (*slang*)

Party hardy! (*slang*)

418   Asking about the time that a bar closes

Is it closing time already?
Last call already?
> last call = the announcement of the last opportunity to purchase a
> drink before closing time

When do we have to be out of here?
When's last call?

419   Encouraging someone to finish a drink

Drain it.
Drink up.
Have one for the road.
Pound it and let's go. (*slang*)

420   Drinking toasts

Here's looking at you.
Here's mud in your eye.
Here's to you.
Here's to us.
To your health!
To John V. Jones!
Cheers!
Down the hatch!
Bottoms up!
Drink up!
To life!

421   When someone drinks too much

I think that this is your last one.
I think you've had enough.
That's all for you, Bud. (*informal*)

Haven't you had about enough?

Do you really think you ought to have another one?

422   Stating that someone is drunk

He's feeling no pain. (*informal*)

He's drunk as a skunk. (*informal*)

He's three sheets to the wind. (*informal*)

He's stone drunk.

He's tanked. (*slang*)

He's pickled. (*slang*)

He's as drunk as a lord. (*informal*)

Home Cooking

423   Stating that you are hungry

I'm hungry.

I'm famished.

I'm starved.

I'm ravenous.

My mouth is watering.

That stew is mouthwatering.

I'm so hungry I could eat a horse.

I could eat a horse. (*cliché*)

I'm (just) dying of hunger.

424   Asking when a meal will be ready

When do we eat?

When's chow? (*slang*)

When's dinner?

When's supper?

When will supper be ready?

425   Asking what is for dinner

What's to eat?
What's for supper?
What are we having?

426   Stating when food will be ready

Dinner's almost ready.
It's almost done.
It will be on the table in a minute.
It's almost ready.
(It's) time to eat.
It's time to sit down.
Dinner's ready.
Please be seated at the table.
Dinner is served. (*formal*)
Soup's on! (*informal*)
     = *Dinner's ready!*

427   Offering someone a bit of food

Would you like a taste?
How about a bite?
Would you like a bite?
Want a taste?

> How about a bite?

428   Blessing the food

Who wants to say grace?
Shall we say grace? (*formal*)
Shall we pray? (*formal*)
Let's pray.
Let us pray. (*formal*)

429   Concerning passing food at the table

Please pass me the salt.
Please pass the pepper.
Please pass the butter.
Could you pass the rolls around?
Could you start the rolls around?
Could you start the rolls going around?
Could I have some gravy?
Would you like the salt and pepper?
Would you care for the butter?
Would you care for some butter?
Pardon my boardinghouse reach. (*informal*)
    boardinghouse reach = a long and somewhat impolite reach for
       something at the table

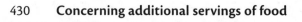

430   Concerning additional servings of food

Could you pour me some more milk?
More milk, please.
Could I have seconds, please?
May I have seconds, please?
Would you like some more of this?
Is there any more of this?
What's for dessert?

431   Enforcing good table manners

Don't put your elbows on the table.
Don't talk with your mouth full.
Don't read at the table.
No TV during dinner.
    TV = television
No texting at the table.
Turn that cell phone off.

Wipe your mouth.

Put your napkin on your lap.

Put your napkin in your lap.

432   Cleaning up after a meal

Can you help me with the dishes?

Please carry your own dishes to the kitchen.

I'll wash and you dry.

I'll scrape and you load (the dishwasher).

433   Excusing oneself from the table

May I be excused?

Do you mind if I leave the table?
  (said by an adult)

I'll have to excuse myself.
  (said by an adult)

May I please leave the table?
  (said by a child)

May I be excused?
  (said by a child)

434   Encouraging children to eat

Finish your food.

Be quiet and eat your dinner.

Be quiet and eat your food.

You have to clean up your plate.

If you don't eat your vegetables, you won't get any dessert.

There are starving children in Africa. *(cliché)*

  Africa = Bosnia, Asia, South America, etc.

SHOPPING

Stores and Shops

435 Asking about store hours

When are you open?

When do you open?

How late are you open (today)?

What are your hours?

Are you open on weekends?

Are you open on Saturday?

Are you open after five?

436 A salesperson greeting a customer

Can I help you with something?

May I help you?

Can I help you?

Can I help you find something?

Can I help you with something?

Can I show you something?

Are you being helped?

Is someone waiting on you?

Is there anything I can help you with?

Is there anything I can help you with today?

Is there anything I can help you find today?

437 A salesperson offering help to a customer

If you need me, I'll be right here.

If you need any help, I'll be right here.

If you need me, my name's Linda.

If you need any help, my name's Linda.

If I can help you find anything, I'll be right over here.

If I can help you, just let me know.

There's a mirror over there.

The changing rooms are over there.

Only six items in the dressing room at a time.

Only six items allowed in the dressing rooms.

438 Questions a salesperson might ask a customer

What are you interested in?

Are you looking for something in particular?

Are you looking for anything in particular?

Do you have anything in mind?

Do you have something specific in mind?

Do you know what you want?

What size do you need?

Do you know what size you are?

439 Offering merchandise to a customer

I've got just what you're looking for!

I've got just your size.

I've got just what you're looking for.

I've got exactly what you need.

I have just the thing.

    just the thing = exactly the right thing

Have I got something for you! (*informal*)

May I suggest this?

That's on sale this week.

440 Offering additional help to a customer

Do you need anything to go with that?

Is there anything else I can interest you in?

Is there anything else I can get for you?

Is there anything else I can help you with?

What else can I do for you?

441 Finding things in a department store

Where is the men's shop?
Where is ladies' wear?
    ladies' wear = women's clothing department

Where is the shoe department?
What floor is furniture on?
Where are the children's clothes?
Where's children's clothes? *(informal)*
Where can I find children's clothes?
Do you sell appliances here?
Where is the credit department?
Is there a public restroom here?

442 Shopping for something at a department store

I'm looking for something for my wife.
I'm looking for something for my husband.
It's a gift.
I need a size 34.
I don't know my size.
Can you measure me?
Would you measure my waist, please?
I need a belt.
I need some jeans.
I need a pair of pants.
I need socks.
I need a pair of socks.
I need gloves.
I need a pair of gloves.
I need a bathing suit.
I need a swimsuit.

I'm looking for something for my wife.

443 When you are just looking and not buying

I'm just browsing.
Thank you, I'm just looking.
Just looking.

444 Choosing merchandise in a store

I just can't make up my mind.
I'm not sure which I like.
Which do you prefer?

445 Questions a customer might ask in a store

Do you have this in blue?
Do you have this in suede?
Do you have this in wool?
Do you have this in a larger size?
Do you have this in a smaller size?
Do you have something a bit
   less expensive?
Do you have anything
   less expensive?
Got anything cheaper? (*informal*)
Do you have this in stock?
Do you have any more of these?
Do you have a shirt to match this?
Do you have a shirt to match?

Do you have anything less expensive?

446 When a customer wants to try on clothing

I'd like to try this on.
I want to try this on.
Can I try these on?
Where is the fitting room?
How many items can I take in the dressing room?

447   Encouraging remarks a salesperson might make to a customer

That looks nice on you.
That looks great on you.
That's your color.
This is you!
It's you!
That's you!
That flatters you.
That's very flattering.
That really flatters your figure.

448   Asking how a purchase will be paid for

How would you like to pay for this?
How do you want to pay for this?
Would you like to put that on layaway?

    *layaway = a purchase method where a deposit is made and the
       merchandise is held by the merchant until the balance is paid*

Will that be cash or credit?
Will that be cash or charge?
What method of payment will you use?
Do you have our store card?
Would you like to sign up for our store card?

449   When a salesperson cannot supply exactly what is wanted

We don't have that in your size.
We don't have it in that color.
We're out of that item.
I can back-order that for you.
I can issue you a rain check.
It will be delivered to the store within a week.
We can notify you by phone or e-mail.
You can order it from our website.

450   When merchandise is not satisfactory

It's too tight.

It's too loose.

I don't like the color.

I'll have to keep looking for
    what I want.

It's a little pricey.

    pricey = expensive

It's too expensive.

451   Asking about payment plans in a store

Is it on sale?

Will it be on sale soon?

Is it going on sale soon?

Can I put it on layaway?

    layaway = a purchase method where a deposit is made and the
        merchandise is held by the merchant until the balance is paid

Can you hold it for me?

Will you hold it for me?

Do you have a layaway plan?

Do you take credit?

Can I apply for a credit card?

What financing options do you have?

452   Getting a purchase gift wrapped in a store

Can I get it gift wrapped?

May I get it gift wrapped?

Can I get this gift wrapped?

Where is the gift-wrap counter?

Is there a charge for gift wrapping?

Can you gift wrap that?

Would you please gift wrap that?

TELEPHONES AND MOBILE DEVICES

Answering the Telephone

453   Receiving communications on your mobile device

That's my phone.

It's my ring tone.

I'm being texted.

Do you mind if I take this call?

I need to take this call.

Sorry, do you mind if I take this?

I'll just be a minute.

I just need to send a reply.

I need to text her back.

454   Answering the telephone—residential

Hello.

Smith residence.

Hello, Smith residence.

Yo! (*informal*)

Yeah! (*informal*)

Yes.

John Jones.

Hello, this is John Jones (speaking).

John Jones, may I help you?

John.

John, may I help you?

455   Answering the telephone—business

City Hall. What department please?

Smith Company.

Smith Company, may I help you?

Smithco, how may I direct your call?

456 Asking whom a telephone caller wants to talk to

Who do you want to talk to?

Who do you want to speak with?

Who do you wish to speak to?

Whom do you wish to speak to?

With whom do you wish to speak? (*formal*)

Do you know her extension?

457 Screening someone's telephone calls

May I ask who is calling?

May I tell her who's calling?

May I ask who is calling?

Whom may I say is calling? (*formal*)

Who shall I say is calling?

Whom shall I say is calling? (*formal*)

Who's calling?

Is she expecting your call?

458 Connecting or transferring a telephone caller

Do you wish me to page Mrs. Robins?

I will see if she's in the building.

Let me page her.

Let me connect you with that department.

459 Putting a telephone caller on hold

He is on another line. Will you hold?

Would you care to hold? (*formal*)

Would you like to hold?

Just a moment, please.

Please hold.

Hold, please.

Hold the line. (*informal*)

Can you hold?

460 Interrupting a telephone call with other business

Just a moment; I have another call.

Hang on a moment.

> to hang on = to wait

Hang on a sec(ond).

Just a moment, I have another call.

461 Taking a call off hold

For whom are you holding? (*formal*)

Whom are you holding for? (*formal*)

Who are you holding for?

Who's on the line?

Are you being helped?

Have you been helped?

May I help you?

Can I help you?

462 Offering to take a message from a telephone caller

He's not in; would you like to call back?

She is not available. Can I take a message?

She is away from her desk. Can I take a message?

May I take a message? (*formal*)

Could I take a message?

Could I have someone call you?

463 Offering to help a telephone caller

Is there anyone else who could help you?

I would be happy to try to answer your question.

Would you care to talk to her secretary?

Could I help you?

464   Bringing a telephone call to an end

I have to get back to work before the boss sees me.

I have to get back to my work. I will call again later.

There's someone on the other line. I must say good-bye now.

I really have to go now.

I'll have to take your number and call you back.

Can I call you back? Something
    has come up.

Can we continue this later?

    My other line is ringing.

The doorbell is ringing.

    I'll call you back.